Overnight or Over Time?

OVERNIGHT OR OVER TIME?

Success Stories of the Most
Influential Internet Entrepreneurs

SINA MOEENDARBARI

Contents

Overnight or Over Time?

Introduction

Follow Your Heart

"If you really look closely, most overnight successes took a long time."
—*Steve Jobs*

Google. Amazon. Facebook. These are just a few of the numerous tech startups that have changed how we communicate, socialize, shop, work, and play. The technology they have brought into the world has forever altered the landscape of society, bringing us closer together despite the distance between us and helping to forge a true, globally connected world. And each was created by a bold individual who dared to think outside the box. Within these pages is an inside look at the origin stories of some of the world's most powerful and influential individuals and businesses. But their rise to greatness wasn't always as easy as it looks from the outside.

While these companies are household names today, few people know about their humble beginnings and the fascinating stories of the men and women whose blood, sweat, and tears created the power-house businesses we know today. Who are they? What were their lives like? And how did they take the tiny seeds of their ideas and nurture them into some of the biggest names in tech with the highest net worth?

From college dorm rooms to tiny, cramped offices based out of garages to the bright lights of Silicon Valley, within these pages, you will get an in-depth look into the lives of the now-billionaires who have forever changed the way technology influences our daily lives. Don't be intimidated. Really, they are not so different from you and me. Hailing from across the globe, often with very humble beginnings, what sets them apart is their drive, ambition, and willingness to take risks.

Whether leaving their hometowns and setting out for the big city, dropping out of college to pursue a dream, or whole-heartedly embracing technology the rest of the world has yet to understand, each of them took simple steps day-by-day towards their success. Achieving greatness required hard work, sacrifice, unexpected partnerships, and intense tenacity – working more than 12 hours a day, struggling to make ends meet, fighting against the status quo. And although it may seem they became instant success stories, as you'll see, their accomplishments were often over time... not overnight.

Many of these entrepreneurs faced extreme naysaying from the very beginning. Some struggled desperately to raise funding; others were told their ideas were crazy or impractical. But they had faith in their concepts and would go to any lengths to bring them to fruition. Likewise, many were started by people working entirely outside their realm of academic knowledge. Similarly, many of these self-made individuals immigrated to the US from countries in Asia and Africa, overcoming language barriers and socioeconomic hurdles to get where they are today. Who would have guessed a philosophy student planning on going into academia would become a trailblazer in the technology sector? Or that a Chinese immigrant boy who spent his teenage years washing dishes in a restaurant would create the most popular food delivery service in the US? This only proves that one's background and scholastic aptitude are just the tip of the iceberg and that self-education and passion matter above all else.

While reading their inspirational stories, you will enjoy the excitement these individuals experienced every time they took a chance, and it paid off big. Likewise, feel their pain as they cope with setbacks and failures that could have led them to throw in the towel – but they never did. They faced difficult decisions, sometimes making the wrong ones and struggling to pick up the pieces. But through it all, they persevered, becoming leaders in their field, inspirations to millions – and billionaires – in the process. Their contributions have improved the lives of countless people worldwide, offering solutions to problems that seemed unsolvable, proving that forming a startup isn't just about making money. It's about discovering your passion, following it through, changing the world, and only then reaping the rewards of your efforts.

And these stories go beyond inspiration. If you've ever had a dream that seemed beyond your reach, then this book will provide you with an outline of how to achieve it. It offers practical insight into finding early customers, raising funds, and finding the best product-market fit. It also touches on what makes a business successful and offers marketing tricks, teambuilding techniques, and insight into technical challenges one may face along the way.

While assembling this book, I became deeply engaged in the stories of these entrepreneurs. Their determination and accomplishments ignited my own entrepreneurial spirit, inspiring me to delve into forming my own startup in the hopes of bettering lives and creating the change I want to see in the world myself. I sincerely hope it does the same for you. As Steve Jobs said, "Have the courage to follow your heart and intuition. They somehow already know what you truly want to become. Everything else is secondary."

Chapter 1

You're Like Cockroaches

The Story of Airbnb's Founders

"If you really want to do something, you'll find a way. If not, you'll find an excuse."
—*Jim Rohn*

Airbnb is an online platform where people can list or rent privately owned properties for short-term stays, be it an entire home, a spare bedroom, or even a sofa. Now widely known and used worldwide, Airbnb was originally started in 2008 as "Air Beds and Breakfast" for conference attendees visiting from out-of-town. It all began with three young people, Brian Chesky, Joe Gebbia, and Nathan "Nate" Blecharczyk, in their small apartment in San Francisco, California.

When the time came to go to college, Brian Chesky decided to follow his passion and go to art school to study industrial design. When he told his parents, who were both social workers, about his decision, they warned him that he would have to make sure he could get a job that had health insurance and paid well enough that he wouldn't move back to live in their basement after school.

Brian met Joe Gebbia, who studied industrial design too, in

college. After graduation, Brian and Joe both moved to California, where Brian got a job as an industrial designer for a small firm in Los Angeles, and Joe started working for a book publisher in San Francisco. Brian was unfulfilled in his career, so he decided to do something different after some time living in Los Angeles. He ended up designing a new toilet seat for a finalist on a reality TV show called "American Inventor," produced by the famous TV personality Simon Cowell. The experience of inventing something new, even something as mundane as a toilet seat, got him thinking about finding a new path for his career and life.

Meanwhile, Joe, who always wanted to be an entrepreneur, was amazed by all the startups in San Francisco. In 2007, he finally convinced Brian to move in with him to start their own company. Neither of them had any idea what their product would be, but Brian was still convinced enough to quit his job. He packed up his stuff and drove up to San Francisco in his Honda Civic with only $1000 in his bank account.

As soon as Brian got to San Francisco, Joe told him that the rent of their three-bedroom apartment had just gone up. Since neither of them could really afford the new rent, they realized they either needed to move or make some extra money. Coincidently, the international conference of Industrial Design would soon be in San Francisco. Brian and Joe checked the conference website and noticed that all the hotels listed were sold out. Suddenly they came up with an idea: use the extra space they had in their apartment to create a place for the visiting designers to stay and provide beds and breakfast. They had no bed in the empty bedroom, but Joe was a camper and had three air mattresses. So they came up with the name AirBedandBreakfast.com.

Joe designed and brought up the website in just one day. Then they emailed the top design bloggers to spread the word. People immediately started writing them to ask about staying in their apartment. They hosted three people during the conference; a woman from Boston, a father from Utah, and a graduate student from India. While hosting, Brian and Joe also became friends with their guests. They took them around and showed them around the city, then went to the conference together.

When Brian and Joe saw their simple idea had worked, they became very excited about it and decided to pursue it more seriously as a business. But when they shared it with other people, everyone told them it was the worst idea ever because they didn't think anyone would want to stay with a stranger. Despite the negative feedback, Brian and Joe decided to try to make an enterprise of their idea in the hopes of at least paying rent.

Since Brian and Joe were both designers, they needed the help of an engineer to make a custom website. Fortunately, before Brian moved to San Francisco, Joe was roommates with Nate Blecharczyk, a computer science graduate from Harvard University, until Nate decided to move out when the rent was increased. When Joe told him about their air beds and breakfast idea, Nate found it interesting enough to give it a try and joined Brian and Joe as the third co-founder and CTO of the company.

Brian, Joe, and Nate got together and started working on a platform where people could book stays in homes the same way they could book a hotel room. But because of their initial hosting experience, they first focused on conferences and providing a cheap place for visiting attendees and called the second version of their website "Air-BedsAndConferencesInTheUS." Their new website was more like a directory for events where locals could put up their spare bedrooms, and the travelers coming out of town could look them up and call the hosts to book the room. It took them three weeks to design the website, which they launched for the "South by Southwest" conference in Austin, Texas, in March 2008. However, they only got two customers, one of whom was Brian himself.

After using his own website to stay in someone's home, Brian realized that they needed to add a payment system. They also realized that their service could go beyond conferences and, more obviously, air beds. They changed their site design to make it more general and then launched the third version of their website in the summer of 2008.

The new "Airbnb" version enabled people to book a room anywhere in the world using an online payment system with only three clicks.

Airbnb's co-founders needed to raise money to keep working on it, so Brian reached out to numerous angel investors to seek around $100 thousand, valuing their company at $1.5 million. Some of those investors never responded to their calls, and others refused for different reasons, for example, saying their market was not big enough. Since they could not raise any funds, Brian, Joe, and Nate had no choice but to max out their credit cards, piling up tens of thousands of dollars of debt.

The trio knew that they needed to populate their website with hosts and guests simultaneously, so they started looking for a high-profile event to get press attention. That summer, everyone was talking about DNC, the Democratic National Convention, at which Barak Obama would receive the democratic party nomination for the presidency. DNC would be held in August in Denver and seemed like the perfect opportunity for Airbnb because it would take place in a football stadium that could hold 80000 people, but Denver had less than 30000 hotel rooms.

The Airbnb team contacted CNN, New York Times, and other national news organizations, telling them about their solution for hotel room shortage during the convention. Not surprisingly, all the national press found their idea crazy and ignored them. So, they started reaching out to small bloggers who were more willing to write about Airbnb. The blogs caught the attention of the local newspapers, and they started writing about them as well. In just a week, Airbnb's coverage was picked up by CNN, and they were doing video interviews on a national network. Yet, the excitement quickly wore off; 800 people listed their places on Airbnb, but only about 100 people used it to book a room or house for DNC. Airbnb got almost no bookings the following weekend, even with the media coverage. After three website launches and despite the national news coverage, they were still in thousands of dollars debt with almost no customers. To make matters worse, Nate had gone to Boston to get engaged.

Brian and Joe were desperate to make some money to keep their business going. The presidential election was coming up soon, and Brian and Joe were trying to figure out how to leverage the contact information from the reporters who covered them during the DNC to get more press. Suddenly they came up with the idea of making presidential-themed cereal breakfasts, focusing on the breakfast part of Airbnb!

Brian and Joe made two cereal breakfasts with a presidential theme: one for Barack Obama called "Obama O's, Hope in Every Bowl," and the other one for Republican nominee John McCain called "Cap'n McCain, A Maverick in Every Bite." They did not have the money to order them from cereal producer companies, so they found an alumnus of their college who agreed to print a thousand cereal boxes for free, asking only for royalties. Brian and Joe got the prints in the form of big sheets of cardboard and folded them one by one into boxes. They then went to a supermarket, bought cereal, and stuffed cereal into boxes. Brian and Joe mailed their hand-crafted cereal boxes to the reporters they knew from DNC. Their trick worked, and within a week, they were on CNN again, talking about the presidential cereals. Their interview became the number one political video of the day and was featured on the homepage. The one thousand presential cereal boxes were sold quickly, so they made an additional 400 boxes and started selling them on their website for $40 each. In a week, they sold a total of $30,000 of cereal and used that money to fund their startup.

But it was the beginning of a recession, and their financial situation was getting worse. Soon they ran out of the money they made by selling presidential cereals and were struggling again. They had been working on Airbnb for ten months without jobs or raising any money, and despite trying different things, Airbnb was making only $200 a week. They started asking themselves if they should give up and quit.

Just when Brian and Joe began losing hope, someone advised them to apply to "Y combinator," the renowned startup incubator and early-stage investor in Mountain View, California. Knowing that it was their last chance, they applied to Y Combinator and got an interview. The whole interview lasted just five minutes but did not go very well for Brian and Joe. Within two minutes, Paul Graham, one of Y Combinator's co-founders, said their idea was terrible and tried to convince them to do something else.

As they were walking out, Joe took a box of Obama O's cereal out of his bag and gave it to Paul. Paul was surprised and asked them what it was. They told him the story of the cereal and how they had funded Airbnb with it. Impressed by their perseverance and story, Paul thought maybe they really could convince people to stay in strangers' homes if they were able to make people buy a cereal box for $40, so he let them into the Y Combinator seed funding program. Paul believed that 2009 was like an investment nuclear winter because of the recession, and only the people who were like cockroaches would make it. He told Brian and Joe that their survival proved they were like cockroaches!

After joining Y Combinator, they dedicated three months to exclusively working on Airbnb full time. They realized that, although they had worked hard, they weren't one hundred percent focused yet. Nate moved back to San Francisco from Boston, and they all started living together again and working on Airbnb every day from early morning to midnight.

Paul gave them advice to improve their business and asked them where most of Airbnb's users were; they said New York City. Paul told them to go to New York and meet all their users. They had only twenty to thirty hosts in New York City at that time, so it wouldn't be hard to meet all of them. The problem was that they had very little money to spend on traveling. Despite the cost, the Airbnb team went to New York City and spent four weekends meeting with every one of their hosts. They noticed that their hosts had very bad photos of their properties. The camera phones in 2009 were not very good, so Brian and Joe went back home and borrowed a camera from one of their friends and then went back to NYC and offered their users free high-quality photos of their places. They also opened Airbnb's website, showed them how to use it, and got some feedback to improve it.

Besides helping users improve their profiles, they invited them out to beer and built good relationships with them.

Because of improved image quality, better profile descriptions, and lower prices, suddenly guests from around the world started booking those NYC rentals, and the hosts started making money. They then told their friends about the experience and the money they earned and encouraged them to list their own properties. Frequently, the guests became hosts at home themselves. Airbnb began growing organically through the network of hosts in NYC and the travelers from other parts of the world who stayed in their places. Properties started popping up on Airbnb all over the world, from Barcelona to Hong Kong.

By Y Combinator's demo date, in which startups had to pitch their product and find an investor, Airbnb had become a profitable company. Soon, they were able to raise seed money from notable investors in Silicon Valley. With the new capital, they started holding local events by going city to city around the US and the world to meet with the hosts and educate them, which enlarged their global network. Since then, Airbnb has become one of the most successful pioneers of the sharing economy, transforming the travel and hospitality industry worldwide. Besides economic lodging alternatives and unique experiences, Airbnb has introduced new features to enable its customers to book an activity or experience with a local host.

Despite facing serious challenges at the beginning of 2020 due to the coronavirus global pandemic, which brought the travel industry to a halt, Airbnb regained its strength very soon and became a public company in December 2020 through one of the most successful tech IPOs ever. Airbnb shares ended their first trading day up more than 112%, valuing the company about $86 billion and making its three humble and hardworking co-founders instant billionaires.

Chapter 2

Catching Shrimp

The Story of Alibaba's Founder

"My mom always said life was like a box of chocolates. You never know what you're going to get"
—*Forrest Gump (Forrest Gump, 1994 film)*

Alibaba is often described as a combination of Amazon and eBay, but unlike Amazon, the company does not sell directly to consumers. Instead, it allows users to search the merchandise offered by sellers in thousands of digital stores. Alibaba was founded in 1999 by Jack Ma Yun in his modest apartment in Hangzhou, China.

Jack was born in 1964 in Hangzhou, China. His parents were traditional musician storytellers. As a poor family of six people living on seven dollars a month, they could afford to eat only one chicken each year. Around that time, a cultural revolution was happening in China. After a historic visit to China by US President Richard Nixon in 1972, China and the United States signed an agreement that led China to open its doors to the world. Jack was about eight years old when Nixon visited his city, making it possible for the American public to view images of China for the first time in over two decades.

After Nixon's visit, Hangzhou became one of the first cities that opened to the West, and many American tourists went there. Jack started befriending the foreign visitors and giving them free guided tours around the city, learning English in the process. At the time, there was no place in Hangzhou that would teach speaking English.

For nine years, every day, Jack went to Hangzhou Hotel, where most foreign visitors stayed, and showed them around West Lake, a UNESCO world heritage site. Besides learning English, Jack even got his English name from one of those visitors. Once a lady told him that his Chinese name was difficult to pronounce and asked if he had an English name. He said, "No, give me one." She replied, "OK, my father is called Jack, my husband's name is also Jack, so what do you think about Jack?" He liked it, so Ma Yun became Jack Ma. Besides the language, Jack learned a lot about Western culture and realized that what he was learning from the American visitors was very different from what he had been taught by his parents and school.

Jack could not go to a good school, and despite studying hard, he failed many tests from primary to high school. After failing the national university entrance exam the first time, he started applying for different jobs but was turned down for all of them. He and five of his classmates applied to become police officers. Four of them were accepted, but Jack was rejected. When KFC came to his city for the first time, twenty-four people applied for a job there. Out of them, twenty-three were accepted. Again, Jack was the only one rejected, without even knowing why. When the first 4-star hotel opened in Hangzhou, Jack and his cousin waited for two and half hours in line in the sweltering summer heat to apply to become waiters. Jack's scores in the interview turned out much better than his cousin's, but his cousin got the job, and he did not. Later, he learned that they hired his cousin because he was taller and more handsome. Jack was considered a loser by many because he couldn't get a job.

After three years of attempting to enter the university, Jack finally got into the lowest ranked university in his city, Hangzhou Teachers College, which trained teachers. Jack hated the idea of becoming a teacher because, in China, people considered it a low-level job for men at the time. Every day, for four years during college, he thought about what he would do after graduation. Yet, after graduating, he became a teacher to use government assistance to pay for his college expenses. Jack's college was supposed to train middle school teachers, and there were five hundred graduates each year. Only one graduate per year could be assigned to teach at university instead of middle school, and Jack was chosen among his classmates. The university president told him, "Jack, I know you will leave one day, but promise me you will teach in the university for at least five years." He said, "OK, I promise."

When Jack started his job at the university, he did not know that his salary would be so low; just under $10 a month. Still, he kept his promise and taught there for five years. The students selected him as the best teacher at the university. Jack gradually began to love being a teacher. In his 6th year, he realized everything he was teaching his students was what he had learned from books. He thought if he wanted to be a really good teacher, he should leave the school, spend ten to fifteen years experiencing different things, and then go back to the university to teach again.

In 1995, while Jack was looking for a job outside of the university, he visited the United States to help his city's local government with a project to build a highway. During his trip, he learned about the internet for the first time. One of his friends lived in Seattle and had a small office with a few computers. He told Jack about the internet, but Jack couldn't understand its concept. He suggested Jack search for whatever he wanted, but Jack was afraid he might break something and wouldn't be able to pay for the damage. At the time, computers were extremely expensive in China. His friend said, "Come on, just search for something." Jack searched for beer because it was easy to spell. He saw the web results for beers from Germany, the USA, Japan, and other countries. But there was nothing from China. He then typed "China," and again, nothing appeared. He was surprised and then wondered if they should make something about China on the internet.

Jack and his friend decided to make a small website about Jack's translation agency to see what would happen. They launched their one-page website one morning. By noon, Jack had gotten a phone call from his friend telling him they had already received five emails. Back then, Jack even didn't know what email was. But he soon realized that the internet had a lot of potential, and he should put it to use. On his way back to China, Jack thought it might be good to put Chinese companies' information on the internet to enable other people to find them. He had no idea that the internet would become so big. He just didn't want to be a teacher anymore and was looking for a new job, so he decided to try his idea.

When Jack returned to China, he invited twenty of his friends to his apartment to explain his idea about the internet. After two hours of explaining what he would do with the internet, almost all of them thought it was a stupid idea and told him it would never work. They said there was no such thing as the internet, and even if there was, Jack knew nothing about computers. They questioned why he wanted to do it. Only one person said, "Jack, if you really want to do this, just try it. But if it doesn't work, go back to your teaching job." After thinking for the whole night, Jack decided that he still wanted to do it and the next morning resigned from the university.

For three months, Jack tried to borrow $3,000 from a bank to start his business, but the bank wouldn't give him the money. He then borrowed $2000 from his relatives and friends and created a website called China Pages. Jack went to the registration office to register his company and chose the name "Hangzhou Hope Internet." The officer showed him an English dictionary and said there was no such word and wouldn't let him use the name he wanted. At the time, China was barely connected to the internet. The first-ever internet connection in the country had happened in 1994 at a research institute. Jack was the seventh person or company connected to the internet in the country.

Some started saying that Jack was a liar and was trying to steal money from people by telling them that there was a thing called the internet. To prove that he was telling the truth, he invited one of his friends who worked for a TV network and asked him to bring his camera and some other people to his home to film how the internet worked. It took them about three and half hours to connect from

Hangzhou to Shanghai and then from Shanghai to America and download the first website's front page. During that time, Jack had to make several stories to encourage his friends to stay and see that he wasn't lying.

When Jack started his first company, he didn't know anything about technology or computers, so he sought help from the government officials, but they turned him away, saying that what he was doing wasn't appropriate and he should just go back to teaching English. China Pages failed, so Jack started looking for a job again and, in 1997, joined the Chinese ministry of foreign trades as a contractor. He worked there for a year and a half while the internet was rapidly rising in the United States, and companies like Amazon and eBay were growing very quickly. Jack was still crazy about the internet and thought that if China joined WTO, many Chinese products would be sold across the board. He decided it would be a great idea to make a website that could help Chinese products sell outside the country and connect the small businesses to other parts of the world. With that in mind, Jack started Alibaba in 1999 based out of his small apartment.

Jack created Alibaba with a team of seventeen co-founders; most of them were his students and friends, and none of them were very successful at the time. Among those eighteen people, only three were knowledgeable about computers. Jack and the other co-founders combined their savings to gather $60,000, leaving just enough money for ten months of food and rent for themselves. The day they started Alibaba, Jack told his team in his apartment that they had to work hard not only for themselves but for helping Chinese small businesses. While everyone else thought they didn't have what it took to succeed, Jack believed they had to start doing it right away to prepare for the future when the e-commerce boom would come to China. Jack also told his co-founders that one day their website would be one of the top ten websites in the world, although very few people believed that they would make it happen.

Jack and one of his co-founders went to Silicon Valley and tried to raise money from venture capitalists, but they were rejected by everyone. People even didn't want to hear about what they were doing. Jack told them their story anyway, explaining that they would bring e-commerce to China and become one of the top ten websites. Everyone thought that he was crazy. They said, "None of you eighteen employees have good resumes, the internet is just starting in China, there are no shipping logistics, there are no credit cards, how could you be successful?!" So, they returned to China and continued working with their own money. Finally, a big investment came about one year after Alibaba was founded. Japan's Softbank CEO, Masayoshi Son, visited Beijing to meet with internet startups. All the startups presented very detailed business plans, but Jack Ma got up there with no presentation and just told his story and talked about his vision of what he wanted Alibaba to become. Masayoshi Son got so excited that he pledged to invest as much as forty million dollars in the company. But Jack turned it down and said they only needed twenty million dollars at that time.

In 2000, when the internet was starting to gain traction in China, Alibaba was trying to go global from a small apartment in Hangzhou. Jack was going door to door, telling people they should spend their money to put their company on this thing called the internet. Yet, many Chinese small businesses couldn't see its potential. Alibaba made zero revenue for the first three years. But Jack was still excited about the work he was doing as he saw that they were changing the people's lives. Jack got many emails from their customers who thanked them, saying, "Alibaba is such a great thing. We cannot pay you now, but it has helped us. Please keep it going." Sometimes when he wanted to pay the bill at a restaurant, the owner would come over and say, "Sir, your bill was paid by someone already," and then give him a small note that read, "Hi Mr. Ma, I'm one of your Alibaba customers. I've made money using Alibaba, but I know that you aren't making any money, so I paid the bill for you." Many people showed their appreciation by sending him small gifts.

Around 2002 when the dot-com bubble had burst in the US, Jack was still trying to figure out how to make the internet work for him in China, but thus far had been unsuccessful and was losing his optimism. Coincidentally, Jack visited his friend in Seattle again around the same time. He watched the movie "Forrest Gump" at his friend's home and noticed that Forrest Gump made a fortune by catching shrimp, not catching whales. Jack loved how Forrest Gump was a simple guy who believed in what he was doing, no matter whether other people liked it or not. Jack thought that continuing to help the Chinese small businesses would make him like Forrest Gump. Inspired by the movie, he went back to China to work harder while always remembering what Forrest Gump's mother told him, "Life is like a box of chocolate, you never know what you're going to get."

In 2003, eBay, which had survived the dot-com crash, announced its plan for expansion into China by acquiring a Chinese auction website that dominated China's market share for $180 million. Since Alibaba was a business-to-business marketplace, Jack made a team to create a shopping website, named Taobao, focused on consumer-to-consumer sales like eBay. When they launched Taobao, Jack asked his Alibaba co-founders to go home and look for four things they could list on their website and see who would buy them and how much they sold. But all of them were still poor people and could find very few things to sell online. Still, they gathered what they could and listed their items on their website. But nobody bought anything, and after three days of waiting, they started selling to and buying from each other. The first week all the sales were amongst themselves. A week later, someone tried out selling on their website. For almost thirty days, everything people listed they bought themselves, but as people saw how the website worked, more and more started coming to Taobao and using it. To compete with eBay, Taobao did not charge its users transaction fees and tried instead to make money from online advertising and providing additional services. However, gaining customers' trust was still a challenge because Chinese banking was inefficient at the time, and there was no simple way for people to pay online. Through Jack's industriousness, Alibaba created an online payment system called Alipay to instill confidence in online sales, which was a big deal for the Chinese financial industry. The hard work eventually paid off when Alibaba's Taobao forced eBay out of the Chinese market in 2006.

Over time, Alibaba became a giant holding company with several subsidiaries, including the popular marketplaces Tmall and AliExpress. Jack fulfilled his promise, and now the websites of some of those subsidiaries are among the world's top ten websites. Besides being one of the world's largest retailers, today, Alibaba is also one of the largest cloud and artificial intelligence services providers, competing with companies like Microsoft, Amazon, and Google.

In 2014, Alibaba debuted an IPO on the New York Stock Exchange, which set a record as the largest ever in the United States and gave the company a market value of $168 billion, the highest such value in IPO history for any internet company at that time. Alibaba's enormous value has put Jack Ma among the wealthiest people in China and the world. Jack Ma has said for a long time, "I don't want to die in my office; I'd rather die on the beach." He finally stepped down as the executive chairman of Alibaba in 2019 at age 55.

Chapter 3

Hopelessly Inadequate

The Story of Amazon's Founder

"You're going to figure out one day that it's harder to be kind than clever."
—*Jeff Bezos' Grandfather*

Amazon has become a household name; you can buy anything on its website, from shoes, furniture, and cat toys to eBooks, movies, and music. One-click buying and one-day shipping have made amazon.com one of the most successful online retailers globally. But the retail giant created by Jeff Bezos in 1994 started out in a tiny warehouse as the first online bookstore.

Jeff Bezos was born in Albuquerque, New Mexico, in 1964 to a 17-year-old high school student. Being a pregnant teenager was neither appropriate nor acceptable in Albuquerque at that time. But Jeff's grandfather was very supportive and didn't let the school kick his daughter out. Jeff's mom divorced his biological father and married Miguel Bezos, a Cuban immigrant and petroleum engineer for Exxon, who later adopted Jeff. Jeff spent a lot of time with his grandparents, especially his grandfather, on their ranch in South Texas. From age four to sixteen, he stayed there in the summers. His grandfather made

Jeff believe that he was helping with the ranch work, though he was only a little four-year-old boy. Jeff's grandfather was self-reliant and became one of Jeff's early role models. He fixed prolapsed cattle, did their own veterinary work, repaired windmills, laid water pipelines, and built fences and barns. Jeff learned how to be resourceful from his grandfather's lifestyle.

Jeff fell in love with computers in fourth grade. His elementary school had a teletype that was connected to a mainframe computer. A company in Houston donated a little bit of computer time to that mainframe computer, but none of the teachers knew how to use it. There was a stack of manuals, so Jeff and two other kids stayed after school, taught themselves programming from the books, and figured out how to operate it.

Jeff's love for computers led him to study them in college. In 1986, Jeff graduated from Princeton University with degrees in electrical engineering and computer science. After graduation, a hedge fund recruited Jeff, but he didn't want to work in finance, as he was more interested in computer programming. Still, the firm convinced him to join them because they were working on a specialized kind of investment banking called quantitative hedge fund, built around computer algorithms and the type of technology that Jeff was interested in.

In the spring of 1994, while still working on Wall Street in New York City, Jeff came across a startling fact that astounded him. He noticed that internet usage was growing at 2300 percent a year and became obsessed with that number. Jeff decided to make a business plan in the context of that growth. He realized that the internet was creating new distribution channels, changing how people could buy and sell. So he made a list of twenty different products he might sell online and started looking for the first one. He chose books because there were more items in the book category than any other. In 1994, there were three million different books active in print, while the largest physical bookstores only carried about 150,000 different titles. Jeff realized that he could build something online that no one could create anywhere else; a universal selection of every book ever printed.

Jeff told his boss about his crazy idea to sell books online. His boss said, "This is a great idea, but it would be a better idea for somebody who didn't already have a good job." Jeff's boss convinced him to think about it for two more days. It was a hard decision, but Jeff projected himself into the future and imagined he was 80 years old. Then considered his life and asked himself, "What do I want to have done at that point, so I don't have any regrets?" He immediately realized that when he was 80, there was no chance that he would regret having forgone his 1994 Wall Street bonus. But most likely, he would regret not participating in this fascinating thing called the internet. Even if he tried and failed, he knew he wouldn't regret giving it a shot. So he decided to follow his passion and tell his wife, Mackenzie Scott, about it.

Mackenzie had married Jeff when he was a stable guy working on Wall Street. But a year after their marriage, Jeff said to her, "I want to quit my job and start an internet bookstore." Like everybody else, Mackenzie's first question was, "What's the internet?" Almost nobody knew about the internet in 1994. But even before Mackenzie understood what the internet was, she said, "Great, let's do it." She wanted to support Jeff because she knew that he had always had a passion for invention and longed to start his own company.

Finally, in July 1994, Jeff quit his secure Wall Street job to pursue his dream of creating one of the world's first online bookstores. Jeff's first investors were his parents. When Jeff told them about selling books on the internet, again, their first question was, "What's the internet?" He warned them that it was very likely they would lose their entire investment in the startup. His parents still bet on their son's success and gave him their money.

Jeff had a sense of urgency as he saw the incredibly rapid growth of the internet and wanted to move fast. The problem, however, was deciding where to locate his bookstore. In his opinion, the location was highly constrained by three factors: it had to be in an area with a large pool of technical talent, it had to be in a small state because only the customers who were residents of that state would be charged sales tax, and finally, it had to be near a major book wholesaler. It turned out the largest book warehouse in the world was in Roseburg,

Oregon, so Jeff's attention shifted to the West Coast. He narrowed it down to four cities: Portland in Oregon, Seattle in Washington, Boulder in Colorado, and Lake Tahoe on the Nevada side. Yet, he was unable to decide which would best suit his needs. When the movers came to his house and packed up their belongings, they wanted to know where to take them. Jeff told them, "Just head west and call us tomorrow. We'll tell you then."

In the summer of 1994, Jeff and his wife Mackenzie headed to Washington State armed with $300,000 from his parents. Jeff tapped out the first draft of the business plan in the car on the way. He retained an attorney in Seattle by cell phone to set up bank accounts and incorporate the company. The lawyer asked what the name of the company would be. Jeff said, "Cadabra," but he instantly knew that was a dumb name. The attorney came back to him right away, saying, "What, cadaver?" The guy eventually got it right and incorporated the company as Cadabra Inc. It was hard to choose a name because, even in 1994, most of the good domain names were already gone, but three months later, the name was changed to Amazon.com. Jeff chose Amazon, the name of the Earth's biggest river, because it seemed relevant to the Earth's biggest bookstore.

Jeff and Mackenzie settled in Bellevue, Washington, and rented a house to serve as their first place of business. The house had a garage which became the original office of Amazon.com. The garage was cold, so the owners installed a big pot-bellied stove right in the center to warm it up. Jeff hired two programmers to write the code with him, while Mackenzie, a novelist, took care of accounting. Later, when the fifth person moved into that two-car garage, they moved out the pot-bellied stove, which weighed 800 pounds. It was not an impressive office, so when they wanted to meet with third parties, they would go to a little cafe just down the street. That café was inside a Barnes and Noble store, the biggest bookstore at the time.

Amazon's first office had another problem: there wasn't enough electricity for five team members. The whole garage had only one circuit breaker and was full of computers and other equipment. They had to take long extension cords and run them from every room in the house into the garage. The entire house's power went into the garage to the point where Mackenzie couldn't turn on a hairdryer or vacuum; otherwise, all the computers would turn off. Jeff knew that they really needed to move to a real office to finish up their software development. Finally, they relocated to a small office with about a thousand square feet of space and built their first 400 square foot warehouse in the basement.

Everything was set up by the day before Amazon's launch. But there were no books on the shelves. When one of their programmers looked at that tiny 400-square-foot warehouse, he said, "I can't figure out if this is incredibly optimistic or hopelessly inadequate." Jeff looked at him and said, "We are incredibly optimistic." They planned to use an "almost in time" inventory technique: they would order from wholesalers after customers ordered from them, wholesalers would deliver to them in big boxes, and they would break those big boxes down to ship them out in small boxes. Jeff had very low expectations when starting off and thought it would take a long time for consumer habits to adopt buying online. He felt so strongly about this that he tried to convince the wholesalers to make smaller shipments to them. The minimum shipment size they had to order was ten books, but Jeff was convinced that it would take months before they could sell ten books a day. He tried to get one book, but the wholesalers wouldn't agree to that. Buying from a local bookstore wasn't an option because Jeff wanted to test their planned systems. Luckily, there was a loophole; it turned out that when they ordered ten books, if nine of them were titles that the wholesalers didn't have in stock, they would just ship the one book they had. So, they tested all of their systems by ordering one book and nine copies of an obscure text. It really did seem "hopelessly inadequate."

Amazon.com opened its virtual store to the public in July 1995. Three days after launching, Jeff got an email from one of the Yahoo co-founders. He said, "I saw your website. I think it's incredibly cool, and I'd like to put it on Yahoo.com. But you are going to get a lot of traffic. If this isn't the right time to send all these people to you, let me know, and we can do it in a month or whenever you are ready." Yahoo was still a tiny company at the time, but its website was the most trafficked web page on the internet and was growing exponentially. Jeff and his team discussed it for five minutes and then said, "Let's do it." They got a free opportunity that they'd have to pay Yahoo tens of millions of dollars for in a few months. Amazon's team had programmed a bell so that everybody's computer would ring when they got an order. Then, a little window would pop up, interrupting whatever everyone was doing and showing the order's content. As soon as the Yahoo post hit, suddenly, the bell started ringing constantly and became extremely annoying, so they quickly disabled it.

Nine people worked at Amazon when it was launched, and most of them were software engineers. Everybody in the company, including Jeff, packed books and boxes then shipped them out of their small warehouse. Before hiring more people to do the stocking, they had to work until after midnight, shipping out hundreds of packages every night. They didn't even have packing tables, so they did it all on their hands and knees, sitting on a cement floor. Jeff once said to one of his software engineering colleagues, "This is killing my knees. We need to get knee pads." His colleague looked at him and said, "Jeff, we need to get a packing table." Jeff said, "Oh my God, that is such a good idea." The next day he bought packing tables, which doubled their productivity and saved their backs and knees.

Amazon sold books to customers in all 50 states and 45 other countries within a month. It was still a very small company but was starting to be noticed online. In the first year, they didn't spend a dollar on advertising. People found out about Amazon through word of mouth. In a year, the company reached a revenue of about five million dollars. It was then featured on the front page of The Wall Street Journal as its lead story. That article generated a lot of exposure and awareness for Amazon, and many new customers flocked to the site. However, not only did Amazon's customers read the article, but so did its competitors. It served as a wake-up call for Barnes and Nobles. Jeff was worried about what Barnes & Noble could do with its purchasing power and brand name. He instantly decided that they would have the same prices, no matter how low their profit margins were. It took Barnes and Noble about a year to launch a website following that article. At the same time, Amazon was growing quickly and stayed focused on customer satisfaction.

In May of 1997, Barnes and Nobles launched its website just five days before Amazon's initial public offering. All the headlines at the time were about how Amazon would soon be destroyed by this much larger company. Amazon had 125 employees and $60 million a year in annual sales. In contrast, Barnes and Noble had 30,000 employees and about 3 billion dollars in sales. Yet, that competition didn't concern Amazon. On May 15th, 1997, Amazon's stock began trading on the Nasdaq stock market at $29.25 a share, way above its offering price. Within ten months of Barnes & Noble opening their online bookstore, Amazon's revenue went from $60 million to $260 million a year. Amazon's engineers were hard at work, updating the website by introducing new features like one-click shopping. By the end of 1997, the value of Amazon stock had nearly tripled. Amazon continued its wild expansion, hiring thousands new employees, and started selling whatever it could sell, from cell phone plans and magazines to computer hardware, garden hoses, and toys. Amazon's success led to Jeff being anointed Time magazine's Person of the Year in 1999.

In 2000, the dot-com bubble burst, and stock prices slumped. As a result, many internet companies were forced out of business. By September 2001, Amazon's stock had hit an all-time low, bottoming out at $5.97 a share. Still, Amazon survived that crash and, in 2002, posted a profit for the first time after seven years. Since then, Amazon's stock price and revenue have continued to soar, making Amazon one of the world's most valuable companies. As of 2022, Amazon is among a handful companies in the world that are worth more than one trillion dollars. Besides being one of the largest online marketplaces worldwide, Amazon's constant innovations have made it one of the leaders in artificial intelligence, live-streaming, and cloud computing.

Jeff's estimated net worth increased to over $100 billion in 2017, making him pass Microsoft's co-founder Bill Gates to become the world's wealthiest person. The global coronavirus pandemic caused widespread lockdowns in the United States and most other parts of the world in 2020, which helped Amazon cement its winning position in e-commerce and push its revenue and market capitalization to reach all-time highs. According to Forbes, in summer 2020, Jeff's wealth surpassed $200 billion amid soaring stock prices, making the 56-year-old the world's first-ever person to amass such a fortune. In 2021, Elon Musk, co-founder and CEO of Tesla and SpaceX, surpassed Jeff to become the richest person in the world after Tesla's share price skyrocketed. As of writing this book, Jeff Bezos and Elon Musk have switched places as the world's richest person multiple times.

After running Amazon for more than 25 years, Jeff Bezos stepped down as the CEO in the summer of 2021 and transitioned into the executive chairman's role. Two weeks after leaving his CEO position, Jeff flew to space on a spacecraft made and launched by his own aerospace manufacturer and sub-orbital spaceflight company, Blue Origin. Since then, he has focused on expanding commercial space travel.

Chapter 4

All These Women Are Waiting for You

The Story of Bumble's Founder

"You may kill me with your hatefulness, but still, like air, I'll rise."
—*Maya Angelou*

Bumble is an online dating application where users can create a simple profile with a few photos and a short bio. Then they will immediately enter swiping mode to see people in their area. When someone has a match, it becomes a connection, but only women can make the first move. Whitney Wolf Herd founded Bumble in 2014 in Austin, Texas.

Whitney attended Southern Methodist University, where she majored in international studies and was a sorority member. But she had no idea what she wanted to do after graduating from college, and she was still at home while all her friends were getting excellent jobs in sectors like banking. Every day, her dad asked her, "What's wrong with you? Where's your job? What are you going to do with your life?" She just didn't want to go down the path everybody else was following. She had just come home from Asia, where she had spent time in orphanages. There was no way to connect with others. She was just one person in one room, and the only way to connect to the outside world was through the internet and electronic devices, which inspired her to go into technology.

When she was 22, Whitney joined a startup incubator where she met Sean Rad one night at dinner. Sean said, "I'm starting an app with my friends," and then explained his idea. It sounded like something about consumer loyalty and was not exciting to Whitney. Still, she thought it would at least be a start if she jumped into tech. Whitney told Sean that she could do anything he tasked her with and joined his team. But the project never took off, so they shifted their focus to a small side project they had built during a weekend hackathon. That little project was a dating platform initially called "Matchbox," which later became Tinder.

In 2012, most dating platforms were quite archaic; college students would never use them. But Tinder had a modern and simple design and allowed its users to anonymously like or dislike other users in their area. It was as simple as clicking either a green heart or a red X to select a profile or move to the next one. When two people tapped "like" on each other, Tinder displayed a message saying, "It's a match!" Then, both of them could message each other through the app. Whitney thought that the fraternity guys and the sorority girls on her college campus would love Tinder, so she decided to start there. She would get up on chairs and tables at her old sorority and rally everyone to download Tinder. Then she would run over to the fraternity houses and say, "All these women are waiting for you!" Whitney also dropped all of her fun, cool friends that were still on campus into Tinder match screens, and then printed thousands of copies of those screens and offered some kids twenty bucks to distribute them on campus. Within a week, the entire campus was using Tinder.

When Tinder launched to the public in 2012, it was a near-instant success. The dating app became a sensation on college campuses, which Whitney helped fuel. While working as a VP of marketing at Tinder, Whitney had been dating one of the co-founders. When their relationship broke down, she resigned in 2014 due to growing tensions with other company executives. She then filed a lawsuit against Tinder for sexual harassment, which was settled for just over $1 million.

Whitney's lawsuit against Tinder ended up all over the tech press, but 2014 was still long before the "Me Too" movement went viral. The media coverage of the lawsuit resulted in a difficult time for Whitney. The press painted her as the "gone girl of Silicon Valley." She was just twenty-four years old and was devastated by how the media was treating her. Her dad called her after an unfair article came out about her and asked, "Is this true? Did you really do that?" She said, "No, I promise."

The internet attacked Whitney, and she was abused online by strangers, who even sent her rape and death threats. The constant aggressive behavior made her feel worthless, lose her self-esteem, and have no desire to socialize. Whitney could do nothing about all the online harassment, so she went into a depression for several months. During that time, she was supported by her boyfriend, who later became her husband. Still, she felt she was very much alone in public and didn't want to leave her house or go anywhere.

During those dark moments, Whitney realized that she needed to take control of her life. She decided not to let that situation destroy her and started thinking beyond herself; about people going through something similar. Whitney wanted to solve the problem of online attacks, particularly for women and girls. After much thought, she decided to make a "female-only" social network on which only compliments could be exchanged. There would be no free-flowing negative behavior, and her new social network would not focus on physical attractions but on personality and values.

Whitney started working on the concept and began making her app called "Merci." Around the same time, she unexpectedly got an email from a business person named Andrey Andrew. He was an English-Russian entrepreneur and ran one of the world's largest dating platforms called Badoo. Andrey met Whitney once back in 2013 at a dinner when she was at Tinder and was immediately impressed by her. One year later, when Whitney had that terrible experience at Tinder, Andrey sent Whitney an email and invited her to London. He said, "I have been watching your progression since that dinner. I think we can build a huge business together. Can we talk?" Whitney first responded, "No, I'm not talking to anybody." She still didn't want to leave her house or communicate with anybody, and all her focus was on making her female-only platform. But Andrey insisted, and Whitney's boyfriend told her, "This guy seems very impressive. Why don't you just listen to what he wants to do?"

Finally, Whitney agreed to meet with Andrey, and she and her boyfriend went to London to meet Andrey. When they met, Andrey said to Whitney, "You're going to be my chief marketing officer." She said, "No, I don't want to be that. I can't even leave my house right now! I want to be a founder and do something that is going to change the world." After a lot of back and forth, she pitched him her idea of Merci. Andrey said, "This is amazing. This could be our new dating app!" Whitney said, "No, I'm not working on dating anymore. It is too scary for me." But Andrey believed in her even when others didn't and convinced her to rethink the need for dating to be reformed. Andrey said, "You have such amazing experience from Tinder. Together, we have ten years of experience in building dating platforms. Let's do something together."

Whitney reflected on what she felt was broken in dating and realized that the issue was that women could never make the first move. Women had to sit on the sidelines and wait for the man to initiate conversation. If the woman did do it, she was perceived as too forward and breaking society's rules. On the other hand, she realized that there was a fear of rejection. Men usually felt pressured to make the first move on online dating platforms. And if the woman didn't respond, it would be considered a rejection. But when the woman made the first move, he felt flattered. Whitney thought, "What if we build a platform where only women can say hello and initiate a conversation when two people match?"

Instead of making a platform for females for socializing, Whitney decided to disrupt dating first. In December 2014, she moved to Austin, Texas, and founded Bumble. In this female-focused dating app, only women could initiate a conversation after a match. She and

Andrey partnered to run Bumble like a startup with no need to raise capital. Andrey put up $10 million in seed money for a 79% stake in Bumble. They launched the first version of the app within a few months. It became popular very quickly and reached millions of global users. Over the next few years, Bumble released new features like BFF mode as a way for users to find platonic friends. As of 2022, Bumble is the second-most popular dating app in the US after Tinder.

In 2018, Whitney was named on the Time 100 list before age thirty. Almost a year after becoming a new mom, Whitney led Bumble's IPO as it was listed on Nasdaq in February 2021 with a valuation of more than $13 billion. At age 31, she became the youngest woman to take a company public. According to Forbes, Whitney Wolf Herd also became the world's youngest self-made female billionaire.

Chapter 5

Becoming a Millionaire Before College

The Story of Calm's Founder

"Self-control is strength. Right thought is mastery. Calmness is power."
—*James Allen*

Around the world, people are experiencing unprecedented stress and anxiety in their daily lives. Many have begun seeking their inner peace through mediation and mindfulness techniques to cope with this. Calm is a website and app that provide online meditation tools, including calming exercises, guided meditations, narrated sleep stories, breathing techniques, and health videos. Calm was founded by meditation-enthusiast Alex Tew and his friend Michael Acton Smith in 2012.

In 2005, Alex Tew, a 21-year-old from Wiltshire, England, was about to go to college to study business management, but he was broke and didn't want to get into more debt by taking out a student loan. One night he started brainstorming, trying to come up with an idea to make some money. He wrote down this question on a notepad: "How can I become a millionaire before going to college?" This was quite an ambitious goal, but it sparked a creative process in his mind, and he wrote down the attributes of a perfect idea. It had to be something straightforward, something with a good name that would capture people's attention, and it had to be all about making money. After about twenty minutes, Alex came up with an idea; he decided to sell a million online pixels on the internet for a dollar each!

Alex launched a website named MillionDollarHomepage.com, on which customers could choose from the one million pixels and buy their own for one dollar each. Customers could place advertising logos on the purchased space on his website, linking other users to their own websites. He knew that his idea was crazy enough to capture some attention, but he wasn't sure how much. After selling the first one thousand dollars worth of the pixels to his friends and family, Alex decided to invest that money promoting the website and sent out a press release, which the BBC and popular UK newspapers like The Guardian picked up. On the day the articles came out, he made around two thousand dollars. The next day he made three thousand, and the funds just kept flowing in. He was shocked by the fact that his crazy idea was working and spreading across the internet. MillionDollarHomepage had gone viral before the era of social networks' boom.

The following fall, Alex went to college to study business. But instead of spending his time in the lectures, he was often on the phone doing interviews, running the website, and fulfilling orders. He eventually suspended his courses, thinking that he would later go back to school. Alex was close to earning a million dollars around New Year's Eve, so he put the last thousand pixels on eBay and ran a ten-day eBay auction, and those final thousand pixels sold for thirty-eight thousand dollars. It took him just four and a half months to become a millionaire. After paying the tax and costs for running the project, he bought a place near his parents' home in Wiltshire and invested the rest.

Alex didn't complete his courses and eventually dropped out of the university. He thought it'd be best to capitalize on the opportunities that lay in front of him and became involved in various projects, some of which never quite took off, while others were modestly successful. The next thing Alex tried was another variation of the MillionDollarHomepage. It wasn't an original idea and didn't become as successful as his million-dollar page. However, it generated three-hundred thousand dollars in revenue, which got him to the break-even point. Alex was struggling to be creative for some time. In 2008, he launched "Pop Jam," a comedy-sharing social network for sharing favorite memes and other funny content with one's friends, an idea which ultimately failed.

Around 2009, Alex started thinking about starting a new venture related to mental health and meditation. Since a teenager, meditation had been one of his personal interests, and he had found it very beneficial. Even at that young age, he had considered how to get more people interested in meditation. Some of his friends and family felt Alex's meditation was strange, but it didn't seem so to Alex at all. He thought that if he could create a website for meditation, maybe others would go to it and learn how to meditate, but he buried that idea in his mind until 2009, when he decided to give it a try. Alex wanted to create a platform to make meditation more accessible for modern audiences who were skeptical. He wanted to make a product that he wished he'd had when he started learning to meditate. He had tried to learn meditation by reading books, which he bought from some strange bookshops, or listening to poorly made recordings on CDs and DVDs. Alex wanted his platform to be contemporary, beautifully designed, and without overly spiritual language so people could relate to it in the current busy, modern world.

Alex was very interested in "Calm" as the name for his down-to-earth set of meditation tools, but the domain calm.com had been taken, and the person who owned it wanted a million dollars for it. Alex determined that person lived in Leicestershire, England, so he went to Leicestershire to meet him. The owner had been keeping that domain as an asset and was waiting for his million-dollar payday. Alex didn't have a million dollars, but he stayed in touch with him and negotiated over time, sending him messages like, "Hey, are you ready to sell your domain? I can't do a million dollars, but something more reasonable is possible." It took two years to get that deal through, but eventually, in 2011, the owner sold the domain for 140 thousand dollars to Alex because he hadn't gotten a better offer and wanted to make money.

After buying the domain, Alex and his co-founder Michael Acton Smith started their company, Calm, in San Francisco, California, in 2012. In the beginning, no one believed that a meditation app could succeed, so it was difficult for them to find investors and raise money. Yet, users liked Calm, and it started growing fast. In 2015, it had a revenue of $2.3 million, and by 2017 the revenue reached $22 million. Calm was selected as Apple's "App of the Year" in 2017, and because of that, its cover image was sent out to almost one billion iOS devices. Calm also used celebrities to mainstream meditation, which greatly contributed to its super-fast growth.

In 2020, anxiety levels soared during the global coronavirus pandemic, making meditation apps even more popular. Millions of new paying subscribers got Calm, which helped them deal with anxiety and stress, get better sleep, and improve relationships. As of 2022, Calm's valuation has reached two billion dollars, and the company is looking to do an IPO.

Chapter 6

Can't Stop Reading This

The Story of Coinbase's Founder

"If you don't believe it or don't get it, I don't have the time to try to convince you, sorry."
—*Satoshi Nakamoto*

Bitcoin is digital money native to the internet instead of issued by any country. It was created in 2009 using blockchain technology and can be transferred over the internet almost instantly, like sending an email. One of the easiest ways to get started with digital currencies, also called cryptocurrencies, is to have a wallet to store them. Coinbase, founded by Brian Armstrong in 2012 in the San Fransisco Bay area, has become one of the most popular platforms to buy, sell, or securely store different cryptocurrencies, like Bitcoin, Ethereum, and Dogecoin.

Brian was born in 1983 and grew up in San Jose, California. He was a nerdy kid in high school who started learning Java and CSS by reading books about them. When Brain was in high school, he got his first paying job building websites, and as a teenager, Brian and his friends tried creating startups, like small web design companies. It seemed they had a new business idea every six months.

In 2001, Brian attended Rice University in Houston, Texas, to study computer science and economics. While still a junior student, he co-founded a company to help tutors offer their services to students with his roommate. They set up a bank account, and money began flowing through it. One day, Brian got a call from the bank, asking him questions like, "Are you an aggregator of funds?", "Are you a high-risk merchant?", "Do you have business policy and procedure in place?" and so on. He was scared and felt like he was being treated almost like a criminal.

Brian finished his undergrad with a double major and then got his master's degree in computer science from the same university in 2006. After leaving college, he went to Buenos Aires, Argentina, for a year before returning to the San Francisco Bay Area. He worked a couple years as a consultant for Deloitte in fraud prevention, then later, he joined a couple of startups as a software engineer. One of those startups was Airbnb, a company that operated in 190 countries worldwide. Brian had a front-row seat in witnessing the difficulty of integrating with the global financial system, where every country had its own processes with different fees and delays. While working at those startups, Brain was still thinking of starting his own, and he had put some out on GitHub and launched them on his blog, hoping that one of them would suddenly blow up, which never happened.

Brian was home with his family in San Jose for Christmas in 2010 when he heard about Bitcoin for the first time. He was in his room having a solitary moment, reading Hacker News on the internet when he came across the Bitcoin whitepaper written by a mysterious person named Satoshi Nakamoto; nobody knew his real identity. The paper talked about Bitcoin, a universal currency that ran online. The idea of decentralized, global money and using the internet to move it around the world immediately grabbed Brian's attention. At first, he didn't fully understand that whitepaper, but something about it made him feel that it was the most important thing he had read in the last five years. His mother came to his room and said, "Brian, you need to come down and spend time with the family," but Brian said, "Mom, I can't stop reading this!"

Over the next several months, Brian reread the Bitcoin paper and several other things on that topic many times. Still, it took him a while to finally wrap his head around the concept and realize all of its implications. He couldn't stop thinking about Bitcoin and started going to all Bitcoin meetups in San Francisco. Back then, the Bitcoin community comprised just a dozen people, but he still felt like he was late to the game. After some time, Brian started thinking about creating an online wallet for keeping bitcoins and other cryptocurrencies but found the idea terrifying because he felt a web-based wallet would be a target for hackers.

Brian tried to talk himself out of getting involved with Bitcoin because he knew that he would get completely sucked into it if he went down that path. But eventually, he decided to do an experiment while still working full-time by creating an open-source Android app called "Bitcoin Android" with one of his friends. The app was essentially just a wallet and was designed to store all the data on the phone, so they wouldn't be responsible for safeguarding people's information. After release, the app got a lot of attention, with 15,000 installs in the first couple of weeks. It was translated into German, Russian, and Chinese on Hacker and GitHub, and Wired magazine wrote a little about it. Brian realized that the app validated his idea, and people were really interested in a crypto wallet, which would make it easier to use cryptocurrencies. So, he decided to focus on an easy-to-use, well-designed platform. He also realized that they had built their app wallet in a dead-end way. Because all the data was stored on the phone, they had no way to push updates to them if something went wrong. So he decided to build a reliable cloud-based architecture, taking responsibility for securely storing people's data, which was a service people really needed.

After that experiment, Brian developed a concept that would eventually become Coinbase. But he was still a full-time engineer at Airbnb. His 30th birthday was coming up, and he thought to himself, "I keep telling people that I'm going to start a company, but I'm turning 30 and have not done it yet." That motivated him to finally do it, so in 2012, he started coding a prototype on nights and weekends.

He then applied to Y Combinator, the famous startup incubator in Silicon Vally. Brian claimed that his prototype would be the "PayPal for Bitcoin." He spent three months there working hard to get his prototype ready, then finally launched an early version of Coinbase. Brian and other participants went out on the demo day and tried to raise some seed investments at the end of the Y combinator boot camp. He wanted to raise a million dollars for the seed round, but he could barely get half of that from a couple of angel investors. Many of the venture capitalists he talked to said, "We don't know what this Bitcoin thing is. It sounds like a scam!" It was tough back then, even in Silicon Valley, to raise money for anything related cryptocurrencies.

Because of his past startup experiences, Brian assumed he didn't need a co-founder. He thought if people like Mark Zuckerberg had done it, he could do it too and believed he just needed to build a team of great people behind him. His mindset changed after being at Y Combinator; however, finding the right co-founder and the right team turned out to be very difficult. Brian started going on "co-founder dates." For two years, he met with potential candidates almost every weekend. Afterward, Brian usually thought that person seemed like a good fit, but after the second or third dates, Brian would realize that it would not work for them. He even formed a company with one of them, but they had to break up in the end. It was a very stressful experience, which devastated Brian. Yet, he got back on his feet and began trying to find the right person for the job again.

After much searching, Brian met his co-founder, Fred Ehrsam, the first engineer who joined Coinbase. Fred had studied computer science in college and went to work at Goldman Sachs as an exchange trader in New York after graduation. Meanwhile, he had been reading about Bitcoin on the side. Eventually, Fred took it more seriously, and ultimately, he joined Brian and became Coinbase's co-founder. He was very good at pitching, finance, and product decisions.

Brian and Fred knew that security was the most crucial aspect. They decided to provide security as a service to customers instead of pushing that responsibility off on them. They came up with the idea of disconnecting most of their bitcoins from the internet and storing them offline, so they could not be hacked. Coinbase was also the first company to get private insurance on the bitcoins that it holds. Through those techniques, they eventually were able to provide secure Bitcoin storage.

Since its launch in 2013, Coinbase has grown incredibly fast and has partnered with many major corporations, enabling them to accept cryptocurrency payments. It also launched an exchange for trading Bitcoin and other digital currencies. Coinbase officially filed to go public in February 2021, riding a wave of Bitcoin enthusiasm that skyrocketed the cryptocurrency markets, with an IPO valuation of around $85 billion.

Bitcoin initially traded for next to nothing, and then for some years, its price remained a few dollars. Brian bought his first Bitcoin for around $8. After years of skepticism, Bitcoin finally started gaining mainstream credibility toward the end of 2020. Despite a fluctuating price history, Bitcoin's value has increased tremendously since its creation in 2009. Interest in Bitcoin and other cryptocurrencies soared during the coronavirus pandemic in 2020, and by the middle of 2021, Bitcoin's price reached close to $70,000.

Chapter 7

Machine Learning Class

The Story of Coursera's Founders

"Everyone has the right to education."
—*The Universal Declaration of Human Rights*

Coursera offers online courses from top universities worldwide, which one can sign up to take on their website. Students attend weekly lectures and are given homework to submit and get feedback on. For most classes, if someone finishes the course and meets the grading bar, they will also receive a certificate that can be used to find a job. These online courses could also potentially earn academic credit and transfer towards a degree into a university. Coursera was founded by two Stanford professors, Andrew Ng and Daphne Koller, in 2011.

Andrew Ng was born in the UK to immigrant parents from Hong Kong. His family moved back to Asia and spent several years in Hong Kong and then in Singapore, where Andrew grew up. He was fascinated by computers and started learning to code when he was around six years old. He learned a basic programming language from a book and made simple games by copying code into his computer.

When Andrew was a teenager, his father gave him some books

about artificial neural networks. Andrew thought it was amazing that computers not only would do what they are told to do, but they could also exhibit intelligence and learn to do new things by themselves. He started thinking about how to automate different things using artificial intelligence. In high school in Singapore, Andrew did an internship as an office assistant where he had to do a lot of photocopying and thought, "This is a lot of photocopying. It would be awesome if I could write software or build a robot to automate this."

In 1997, Andrew earned his undergraduate degree with a triple major in computer science, statistics, and economics from Carnegie Mellon University in Pittsburgh, Pennsylvania. He then went to MIT intending to get his PhD, but instead, he earned his master's degree and transferred to UC Berkeley in California to continue his studies. His PhD thesis was on machine learning algorithms, or how computers can learn independently without being explicitly told what to do.

After finishing graduate school in 2002, Andrew started working as an Assistant Professor at Stanford University. One of the classes he taught at Stanford was "Machine Learning," a very popular class that about 400 students would take every year. After a few years of teaching that course, Andrew found himself doing the exact same thing every year. He thought, "Why am I doing this? I could just make a video and then spend my time building a deeper relationship with students."

Around the same time, several other Stanford professors were thinking about using online technologies to improve teaching quality and increase its scale. Andrew started discussing online courses with Daphne Koller, another professor in the Department of Computer Science at Stanford. Daphne joined Stanford in 1995 and helped establish the artificial intelligence discipline there. Andrew and Daphne decided to record some of Stanford's courses and put them online for students to see what would happen. They presented their idea to the board of trustees and the various departments at Stanford. Their initiative created a sense of excitement and energy within the Stanford community about the potential of online teaching.

With the university leaders' support, Andrew and Daphne started creating an online experience to replace classroom time. As they were creating online courses for Stanford students, they decided they should make them available to other people anywhere in the world. They knew that many people might never have the opportunity to set foot at a university like Stanford. Andrew had been thinking about the Universal Declaration of Human Rights since he first read it as a young assistant professor. That declaration said everyone has a right to education, and it should be free and equally accessible to all based on merit. Despite the declaration having existed since 1948, education was still limited by geography and socio-economic limitations.

Andrew and Daphne launched three online courses in the fall of 2011, which went viral, with no marketing and PR except a New York Times article. More than a hundred thousand students registered for those courses within a few weeks, which was more people than Stanford could graduate in a decade. After that experiment, Andrew and Daphne realized that they could not go back to their routine teaching and research and felt they needed to do something. After thinking hard about it, they decided to take a leave of absence from Stanford to start an online education company. Andrew and Daphne talked to the president of Stanford about their decision. He was excited about their idea and gave them some seed funding. They started developing the online platform while filming the course videos at night and on weekends. Andrew was inspired by the thought that they could create content to help many people learn about machine learning. They launched Coursera in January of 2012 with the goal was to take the best courses from the best universities and provide them to everyone worldwide for free.

A few months after they opened Coursera, they had hundreds of thousands of students from most countries in the world. Online course contents had been available for a while, but Coursera was different because it provided a real course experience. It would start on a given day, then the students would watch videos weekly and do homework assignments for a real grade, with an actual deadline. Within a year of its launch, sixteen top universities announced partnerships with Coursera. Before Coursera, most people didn't have access to elite universities. Coursera changed that by taking classes from great schools like Stanford, Princeton, Caltech, and many others and putting them online free for anyone to take.

Coursera reached a million students in less than a year, faster than Facebook reached that number when it started expanding from Harvard to other universities. Andrew and Daphne did not expect that kind of growth in learners or the uptake among top universities. To make Coursera a sustainable business, they started charging companies for accreditation and verification. In a decade, the number of courses on Coursera grew from two to over four thousand. Coursera now has English, French, Chinese, Spanish, and Italian courses, making college education more available and accessible to many people. There has been a rapid rise in new user enrollments since the COVID-19 pandemic in 2020, and it is expected that online education growth will be a long-term trend.

Daphne served as co-CEO and President of Coursera for five years and was elected a member of the National Academy of Engineering in 2011 and a fellow of the American Academy of Arts and Sciences in 2014. Daphne later turned to another critical challenge: using artificial intelligence to improve human health, and in 2018, she founded Insitro, a startup that works on utilizing machine learning for drug discovery.

Andrew Ng has been the chairman of the board of Coursera. He was also the founding lead of the Google brain team, which helped Google become a leading artificial intelligence (AI) company. Andrew has recently founded an AI startup incubator to systematically build AI companies with a high success rate and created "Deeplearning.ai" to educate individuals interested in getting into the field. As of 2022, Andrew's online Machine Learning class has reached millions of students around the globe.

Chapter 8

Crushing the Printer Toners

The Story of DoorDash's Founders

"The first man gets the oyster, the second man gets the shell."
—*Andrew Carnegie*

DoorDash is a technology company offering on-demand food delivery services in the United States and other countries. When customers order from nearby restaurants using either the DoorDash app or website, DoorDash's drivers, called Dashers, get a notification to pick up the food from the restaurant and deliver it to them. DoorDash was founded by Tony Xu and his friends at Stanford University in 2013.

Born in China, Tony Xu moved to the United States with his family when he was still a child. Tony's father went to school in Champaign, Illinois, and Tony was one of only a handful of Asian kids growing up in his tiny college town. They had come to the US with about $300 in the bank, and his dad paid his way through graduate school by working 40 hours a week as a waiter at a restaurant on campus until he got his PhD. After graduating, he became a professor with tenure at the university.

Tony's mother was a doctor in China, but her license was not recognized when they emigrated to the US. Since they didn't have the money to put her through school, she worked as a waitress for twelve years to save enough money to open up a medical clinic. She had to learn medicine in English and how to open a business at the same time. To help his mother, Tony became a dishwasher inside her restaurant when he was nine, which he did for seven years. This gave him the chance to see what running a restaurant was like.

Tony didn't think he would ever make his way out of Illinois. Typically, the kids stayed in Champaign and went to the university there. Then suddenly, everything changed when Tony was in high school; experiencing a midlife crisis, Tony's father decided to leave academia and take up a new career. He drove across the country to the San Francisco Bay Area, California, walked up to the reception desk at Intel, and asked for a job application. Two days later, he got a job, and Tony's family all moved to the Bay Area.

A couple of years later, Tony was accepted into the industrial engineering program at the University of California in Berkeley, the best public school in the area. Ironically, he didn't know what precisely industrial engineering was. He liked math and had applied to the math program, but the industrial engineering program had just moved out of the Math Department into the Engineering School. Someone convinced him last minute that some other courses might be more interesting.

Tony pursued many different things in college, including cancer research, which he considered pursuing a graduate degree in. Yet, near his graduation day, he decided to decline that path, despite having no other alternative. After graduation, most of Tony's classmates would become engineers at companies like Google and Facebook in the Bay Area. But one of his friends got a job at McKinsey, the prominent business management consulting company, and convinced Tony to join the firm too.

Tony didn't know anything about McKinsey, which intrigued him. He showed up in a T-shirt and jeans on day one, which was not the norm, so the recruiting team took him shopping for clothes at Macy's. Although Tony had joined McKinsey on a whim, it turned out to be an excellent training ground for business for him. At McKinsey, he got the chance to work in different industry sectors like technology, airlines, nonprofits, and hospitals. Working at McKinsey taught him how to take a big problem, break it into its components, communicate those parts to different people within a company, and finally turn it into something valuable.

During his work on a McKinsey project, Tony came to know Bob Swan, who was the CFO of eBay and PayPal back then. Tony wanted to follow great people and was impressed by Bob, so in 2009, he decided to join eBay, where he was introduced to the world of startups. At the time, eBay was trying to decide what to do about mobile devices. The App Store had come out in 2008, and a year later, all large companies were trying to figure out their mobile strategy. eBay was looking at some smaller companies for potential investing or acquisition, and Tony's job was to study hundreds of those companies. Tony's group at eBay acquired a company that had an app to scan the barcodes of products and then find them for the lowest price. After the acquisition, Tony was asked to run that business for eBay, his first real entrepreneurial experience. He and his team took the app from a small download base of 50,000 users to about 12 million actual weekly users in a year.

After some time, Tony decided to take a break from working and go to business school. It was more of an opportunity for learning soft skills rather than the business for him. He got into the MBA program at Stanford University, and at the same time, took a part-time job at Square, which then was a small startup of about 100 people. All his classmates thought Tony would most likely drop out in the first year of business school because he was considering working full-time at Square. But before he almost dropped out in the summer between his first and second years of school, Tony and some friends at Stanford decided to work on their own idea.

Tony and his friends, Andy Fang, Stanley Tang, and Evan Moore, who all had computer or business backgrounds, spoke with several local business owners and realized that delivery was a problem for most of them. Some business owners were turning down ten to fifteen orders every week because they required delivery. Tony and his friends could not figure out why no one provided a simple thing like a delivery service. They thought, "When there is not a business, it's typically because no one needs it or no one cares about it." To figure that out, they decided to run an experiment.

Tony and his friends built a website called PaloAltoDelivery.com. It wasn't the best name but was an inexpensive URL they could buy and register in minutes. The website was eight PDF menus of local restaurants in Palo Alto and a Google Voice number that rang their personal cellphones. They wanted to test if people would be interested in ordering from restaurants that had never offered delivery before. Within 45 minutes of launching their website, someone called to order food. They hadn't paid anything for advertising, so they thought the only way this individual could have found them was by typing "Palo Alto delivery" into the browser.

PaloAltoDelivery.com was open only on the weekend and weeknights from 6:00 to 9:00 p.m. because they all were students and had class during the day. When someone called that Google Voice number, one of them acted as a dispatcher who would take the customer's phone call, jot it down in a Google spreadsheet, and then place a pickup order at the restaurant; the rest were delivery drivers. They did the first couple hundred deliveries themselves. On the nights when most of them had class, just one person had to do everything; taking phone calls from customers while riding to deliver orders.

None of them had any marketing experience, so they had to figure out how to spread the word. Tony spent late afternoons delivering food in his 2001 Honda, and in the evening, he raided printer toners of Stanford's campus. Every night from 10:00 p.m. to 2:00 a.m., Tony could be found in one of the rooms on campus, draining the colored printer toners, baffling the librarians coming to work the next day. They printed out over 110,000 copies of half-page fliers for new restaurants with delivery service during that summer.

After running that experiment for a while, Tony and his friends decided to start their own company, DoorDash, out of a two-bedroom house in Mountain View, California, with furniture they bought for $2,000 from Ikea. On a whim, they decided to apply to Y Combinator, the famous startup accelerator program. Shortly after, they received a phone call that said, "Congratulations! You have been accepted into Y Combinator's program. You need to tell us whether or not you want to accept by the end of the day." They decided to join the three-month program and received $120,000 from Y Combinator in exchange for a 7% stake. Tony became Door Dash's CEO.

However, DoorDash was not the most successful startup on Y Combinator's demo day, which was the program's culmination. Most of their peer startups had raised their seed rounds in a week or two, but DoorDash didn't have many food orders per day when they graduated from Y Combinator, thus they struggled to find investors. They were 10 weeks in and had about $10,000 left of cash in the bank and would run out of money very soon even though they didn't pay themselves at that time. It was particularly stressful for Tony because he needed to find a way to pay for his wedding in four weeks. Still, all DoorDash co-founders had enough confidence and conviction based on their experiment that they thought it made sense to continue.

After some struggle, the DoorDash team was finally able to raise their seed funding round, and they then started thinking about their next milestone. They wanted to see if delivery was only a problem for big cities like New York and San Francisco or if there was a demand for delivery everywhere. The first place they launched DoorDash was in a few neighborhoods of East San Jose, California. It was the closest market that could tell them whether their idea could be mass-marketed. It turned out that there was undoubtedly a demand for food delivery services everywhere.

Tony and his co-founders kept delivering food every day, Monday through Sunday, for the company's first six months. They learned about waiting times, the cooling of different foods, parking tricks, and many other small things through those deliveries. They grew from four people in a small apartment on campus to thousands of people spread across hundreds of cities across the US and Canada in a few years.

Since the summer it was launched, DoorDash rapidly grew in the fiercely competitive US food delivery market with other major players like Uber Eats and Grubhub. Despite the competition, DoorDash continued its growth and surpassed Grubhub for the first time in 2019 to become the country's biggest food delivery app in terms of sales. During the coronavirus pandemic in 2020, the demand for delivery services skyrocketed, prompting DoorDash to expand beyond food delivery and include household essentials from convenience stores. When DoorDash went public through an IPO in 2020, its stock soared 85% above its IPO price in its Wall Street debut, valuing the company at around $70 billion. As of 2022, DoorDash still has Tony Xu as its CEO and is the US's most popular food delivery service.

Chapter 9

On the Bus

The Story of Dropbox's Founders

"You are the average of the five people you spend the most time with."
—Jim Rohn

Dropbox is a popular cloud storage service that enables people to back up and share their files online "in the cloud." This means users can conveniently access their files anywhere, like their desktop, tablet, and smartphones. Today, storing data online is very common for general consumers and enterprises alike, but in 2007 when Drew Houston and Arash Ferdowsi founded Dropbox, accessing the data stored online was neither easy nor cheap.

Drew Houston was born in Acton, Massachusetts, in 1983. He was three years old when his parents got their first computer. He loved playing games on it, but eventually, he became curious about how the computer worked. His dad was an electrical engineer, and he helped Drew learn some simple codding. The first line of code Drew wrote with his dad was a program that would ask about someone's favorite color. Even as a kid, Drew knew that he wanted to start a company one day, mainly to design games.

Drew grew to love programming and started beta testing an

online game as a teenager. The game was just getting started, but the company was taking forever to complete it. Andrew grew bored, and with nothing to do, he began poking around to see how the game worked and discovered a lot of security problems. He emailed the game developers and said, "You should look into these broken things, and here are some ways to fix them." They replied, "We'd love some help with this. Would you like to work here?" Drew told them over chat that he was totally in. But he was just fourteen, and the game developers were in Colorado while he was in suburb Boston. He managed to get them to email him all the paperwork, then started working with the company and received a percentage of it. Ultimately, his stake was worth nothing because that startup failed, but he learned many things from his first startup experience.

A couple of years later, Drew decided to go to MIT to study computer science. Besides programming, he was also fascinated with the world of business. Every summer, he lived in his fraternity house, which had a room with a ladder that went up to the roof. Every weekend he'd drag his folding chair and the books he'd bought from Amazon up to the roof and read about different things, like sales, marketing, and strategy management. Initially, he knew nothing about these subjects, and his plan was to keep reading until he learned as much as an MBA on the roof.

In 2004, at age 21, Drew started an online SAT prep company with one of his friends at MIT. Their company strove to make a new type of online course for the SAT. Most high school students used old-school books with hundreds of pages back then. The available online courses weren't very good, so they thought their idea was a big deal. Things were good for a while, but they started going downhill a couple of years later, and eventually, Drew thought, "My God, I just can't deal with any more math questions." Starting a company had been his dream for a long time, so he felt guilty that he was so unproductive. He thought, "Maybe I don't have what it takes after all," and took a little break. But he just couldn't stop thinking about his dreams of becoming a business owner and started working on his startup again.

Drew graduated from MIT in 2006 with a degree in computer science. The summer after his graduation, two of his best friends started a company together. They decided to work out of the same apartment to save some money. They all worked every waking hour. But his friends kept getting pulled away to meet with investors, one of whom even took them on a helicopter ride, which made Drew think, "I have been working on my company for two years, and they have been at it for only about two months. Why can't I meet with any investors?"

Around the end of that summer, his friends told Drew they were moving out to the San Francisco Bay Area. They had gotten some funding from Y Combinator, the famous startup incubator in Silicon Valley. Every now and then, Drew called his friends in San Francisco to see how everything was going, and things were always pretty good. His friends talked to billionaires and famous entrepreneurs who Drew had only read about. Then, one afternoon when he called them, they said they had met with Vinod Khosla, one of the most famous investors in Silicon Valley, who had agreed to invest five million dollars in their startup. Drew was happy for his friends but wondered how his younger fraternity brothers could be so successful while he couldn't get any traction. He thought if his friends could do it, he could do it too and decided to apply to Y Combinator, but his application was rejected. Drew had been working on his SAT prep company for almost three years part-time, but he realized he even hadn't asked himself what would happen in the best scenario; he had no idea what he was doing and wasn't really excited about it.

Drew lived in Boston after he graduated from MIT and decided to visit his friends in New York City for the weekend. It was a four-hour bus drive to NYC, but he justified the long drive by promising himself that he would get a lot of stuff done on the way and made a checklist of things he was going to do. Drew had been running late, and as he sat on the bus and opened his laptop, he suddenly realized that he had left his USB flash drive on his desk at home. All his company's files were on that little thing. He thought, "I'm such an idiot. Why can't I be more organized?" Drew decided to fix that problem, at least for himself. He thought for about ten minutes and then started writing some code, which would become the beginning of Dropbox.

At first, Drew had no idea what his code would turn into, but he was so frustrated that nobody had really solved the problem of easy access to data. Like other people at the time, he emailed himself his files to have them in his inbox. Drew later found an article about all the available online solutions, which he tried but was surprised that none effectively solved the problem. He realized that several websites and apps were needed to upload and back up his files and then sync them across his computers. Drew was convinced that a better solution was really needed and came up with the idea of creating something to access his files and data from any devices connected to the internet, so he wouldn't have to worry about forgetting his USB drive again.

Drew made a prototype of his idea in November 2006 and then applied to Y Combinator again with his new business plan. Shortly after applying, Paul Graham, one of Y Combinator's co-founders and managers, sent an email to him saying, "You are a single founder. You really need to find a co-founder to have a chance here." When the application deadline was drawing very close, Drew still didn't have a co-founder. So he went out to the Bay Area for a weekend to figure out something. He stayed in an apartment building where many Y Combinator companies were and spent the whole time complaining to anybody who would listen that he needed a co-founder. He also showed them some early demos of Dropbox and asked for feedback. One of the people he met told him to go and ask Paul Graham what he thought about his idea.

Y Combinator had dinners for participants every Tuesday at its headquarter in Mountain View. Drew had heard that Paul was usually there early before all the other founders showed up. So, he drove to Mountain View and arrived a little bit before the dinner started. He went to Paul with his laptop and said, "Hey Paul, sorry to bother you, do you have a second? I just want to show you something". Paul said, "No, I'm busy." Andrew insisted, "I'm really sorry, but I'm flying out tonight. It'll only take a minute." But Paul again said, "No, I'm sorry, I don't have time. The whole reason that we have an application process here is so random people don't show up and pitch demos." Disappointed, Drew left and drove back up to San Francisco.

On the flight back to Boston, Drew thought it was over. He was distraught because he thought his idea was very good, and he had a prototype that was working, but he still didn't have a co-founder, and there were only two weeks left to the deadline. Then an idea occurred to him. He made a short video showing the prototype and explaining Dropbox's concept and put the video on Hacker News because he knew that Paul Graham most probably read it there. The video hit the top of the website and stayed there at number one for a couple of days.

One of the people who saw the video was Arash Ferdowsi, an MIT computer science student. Arash emailed Drew and said, "Hey, I saw your video. I think we should talk." Drew remembered hearing about Arash when he complained about not having a co-founder to one of his friends who knew Arash and had suggested he talk to him. So, Drew spent two hours in the MIT student center with Arash, who seemed to be a quiet yet brilliant guy. Everything Arash said seemed reasonable to Drew, and he had no qualms about dropping out of school since he was bored at school anyway and thought quitting was necessary to work on a startup full time. They became co-founders on the spot.

Drew and Arash got into Y Combinator and spent the whole summer doing nothing but writing code from morning to night for ninety days straight. They flew to the Bay Area to pitch Dropbox at Y Combinator's demo day and talk to investors at the end of the summer. But the first thing that everybody told them was, "There are a hundred of these things already. Don't you have any better ideas?" But when Drew asked them if they had used any of them, they would say not really, which made him think that just because many people were working on something didn't mean the problem was solved.

After Drew and Arash wrapped up their presentation on the demo day, someone ran up to Arash and started speaking Farsi, the Persian language, to him. The man's name was Pejman, and he was

Iranian like Arash. Pejman said, "I'd love to talk more with you guys about investing in your company; you should come down to my office in Palo Alto." Drew was thinking, "Who is this guy? I've never even heard of his firm." Their schedule was also very tight because they had come from Boston and would be returning in two days. But Pejman was very persistent, so they finally agreed to go down to Palo Alto. Pejman gave them the address of the meeting spot.

When Drew and Arash showed up, they found out that it was a rug shop! They said to the receptionist, "Hey, we're here to see Pejman." The receptionist took them to the back of the shop, where there was a board room with a tv and projector. Pejman greeted them very warmly and said, "I really like you guys. I want to introduce you to some people at Google, Microsoft, and investors at Sequoia Capital." But Drew and Arash said they were not ready for that because they didn't have any reasonable business plan yet, and their product was still a prototype. But Pejman insisted that they should at least meet with them, so Arash and Drew finally agreed to have the meeting to build their relationship. Pejman got on the phone and set up a meeting with Sequoia Capital. The next thing they knew was that they were at Sequoia's office. When Drew and Arash looked around, they saw pictures of Steve Jobs, Google co-founders, Cisco's founder, and so on. It was very intimidating, but they went to the interview room and did a presentation about data storage, and how keeping it safe was a hassle, and how Dropbox could solve that problem. They then left for Boston.

Not long after, Drew and Arash decided to move to the Bay Area and build their company in the country's tech hub, Silicon Valley. They got an apartment in San Francisco and had just recently moved in when they received a phone call from Sequoia Capital. The person on the phone said, "I like you guys, and I want you to meet with one of our partners, Mike Morse. But there is one problem; Mike is going out of town. Can he come by tomorrow morning?" Mike Morse was a board member of Google and a prominent investor in Silicon Valley. Drew knew the meeting would be advantageous, so he said, "Of course, we're on the north beach. There are a lot of great coffee shops around here, or you could come by the Dropbox headquarter in our apartment." The man said, "That sounds great. We'll see you in your apartment tomorrow at 10 am." Drew and Arash met with Mike Morse in their apartment the following day and ran through their pitch. Afterward, Mike asked a couple of questions, then smiled and left. A few days later, they were invited to the pitch day at Sequoia Capital. After their presentation, Sequoia Capital decided to invest about a million dollars in Dropbox the same day. Drew and Arash were elated but had never had that much money and didn't even know if they could transfer it into their account.

Dropbox was officially launched in 2008. After its inception, it saw steady user growth, obtaining one million registered users in a year and hitting the 100 million registered users milestone 4 years after its launch. As of 2022, Dropbox has hundreds of millions of registered users and generates billions of dollars in annual revenue. The company filed for an IPO in February 2018 and had a market cap of close to nine billion dollars, making it one of Y Combinator's most successful investments to date.

Chapter 10

Broken Laser Pointer

The Story of eBay's Founder

"Everyone is a genius. But if you judge a fish by its ability to climb a tree, it will live its whole life believing that it is stupid."
—*Albert Einstein*

EBay is one of the most popular online shopping sites, best known for its auctions and consumer-to-consumer sales. Anyone can open an eBay account for free and use it to buy and sell almost anything. Now one of the most common online marketplaces, eBay was started as a side project by Pierre Omidyar in 1995 in San Jose, California.

Pierre was born in 1967 in Paris, France, to Iranian parents who had moved there for higher education. He lived in France until he was six years old and went to a bilingual school to learn English. At age six, Pierre moved with his family to the United States, where his father was a surgeon at Johns Hopkins University in Baltimore, Maryland. Because of his father's work, Pierre and his family moved around the United States every two to three years. Pierre's mom and dad separated when he was still very young, so he lived with his mom, but his dad was always around and part of his life. He spent a lot of time on weekends with his dad in the car going from one hospital to the next while having conversations about history, art, science, and many other things. There weren't many kids around him growing up, so he hung out with adults and became mature quickly.

Pierre saw a computer for the first time at school in third grade. He quickly learned how to do a basic program and cut gym time to sneak into the computer room and play on the computer. Pierre wasn't a good student, but he was always willing to try different things because he was raised to believe that he could do anything he wanted. He was paid six dollars an hour to write a program to print catalog logs for the school library in high school. When somebody typed information into his program, it would format it how the librarians wanted and print the library cards. He also worked on software to help schedule classes in 10th grade.

Pierre always wanted a career that involved computer engineering and went to Tufts University in Boston to study electrical and computer engineering. However, the engineering program was too difficult for him. He had no interest in chemistry, but he had to take a chemistry class in his second semester of freshman year because it was required for the engineering program. He studied very hard for the midterm test, but when he got a 25 out of 100, he decided to transfer from the engineering college to liberal arts and started doing the pure computer science program. Pierre learned how to program C in one of his classes and then used that ability to teach himself how to program Macintosh. A year before graduating, he got a summer internship in California, working at a startup on Macintosh's software.

Despite his terrible start at college, Pierre's GPA improved every semester during his four years at Tufts University. He finally graduated in 1988 with a GPA of almost 3.0 and moved to California to pursue his passion for creating software that could benefit and impact people. Pierre was hired at a subsidiary of Apple, where he worked developing software for Macintosh. A few years later, in 1991, he co-founded a software startup called "Ink Development," which was later rebranded as an e-commerce company and renamed "eShop Inc."

Pierre kept working as a software engineer for eShop until the end of 1994 when he joined a mobile communication company as a developer. In 1996, Microsoft bought eShop for about $50 million, and Pierre netted $1 million due to that deal.

The internet was still a brand-new thing in 1995 that nobody was really using at the time except for scientists and academics. Pierre had been watching the internet's development and interactivity. Besides the internet, he had been thinking about how to make markets more efficient for some time. He saw an opportunity for individuals to compete with big companies using the internet. That idea motivated him to do an experiment and make a prototype for an online auction service. At age 28, Pierre started working on his idea as a side project on nights and weekends while he held his day job. He developed a simple website to enable a basic auction for collectible items. He called his platform "AuctionWeb" and launched it online on Labor Day of 1995. The website allowed people to list an item for sale with a title, description, and starting price, and users could also see a list of all the listed things and bid on an item.

To test AuctionWeb, Pierre listed some of his own belongings. The first item sold on his website was a broken laser pointer for less than $15. Pierre was surprised and wondered why anyone would buy a defective product. Still, the buyer assured him that he purposely purchased that broken laser pointer. He was doing a lot of presentations and had seen a couple of laser pointers and wanted one, but couldn't afford a new one because they cost over a hundred dollars at that time. He was an electronics geek, so he thought he'd just buy a broken laser pointer and fix it.

Pierre created a new type of marketplace that didn't exist there before, a place where strangers could do business with one another and exchange merchandise for money without ever meeting. It was a global market for goods usually treated at flea markets and garage sales. His website, however, soon evolved from a flea market into a market for all types of goods. Besides collectibles, the website quickly started selling a vast range of items, including electronics, home appliances, and jewelry.

AuctionWeb grew through word of mouth and quickly became a sensation. Pierre took advantage of that growth by charging a small fee for each transaction, earning a lot of money, which he used to improve and expand his website. Within six months, the revenue he earned paid his costs, and within nine months, the income was more than what he was making at his day job. He realized that his experiment had become a serious business, so he quit his job and focused full time on building his company.

Sometime later, Pierre came up with the idea of creating a commentary form to encourage people to give each other feedback based on how their transaction went. Pierre assumed that most of the responses would be mostly negative because he had been getting a lot of complaints from unhappy customers. So, he wrote a small letter to the community on the feedback forum and said, "We all try to do our best, but sometimes things don't work out. If you're having real problems with somebody, now there's a feedback form so you can post your complaint publicly. But also think about giving praise if somebody does something nice for you." That feedback form became the thing that allowed his platform to succeed, as it gave people a way to trust a complete stranger.

AuctionWeb was growing so fast in 1996 that the whole system could have crashed at any moment. Pierre was racing to stay ahead of the demand, but it was challenging as his website grew twenty to thirty percent every month for the first two years. Everyone believed that there was no way it could continue to grow that fast, but it did. By the middle of that year, the site hosted hundreds of thousands of auctions per day. In 1997, Pierre changed the name of its website and company from AuctionWeb to eBay. A year later, the company filed to go public. As they were preparing for the IPO, they decided to find a way to involve the community in the company's financial success by doing something that had never been done before and creating the eBay Foundation with a grant of pre-IPO stock. Pierre and his business partner Jeffrey Skoll granted one million dollars worth of pre-IPO stock to the eBay Foundation. Shortly after the IPO, that was worth 40 million dollars. Since then, many other private companies have followed this model. eBay's IPO made Pierre a billionaire overnight.

In 1999, eBay expanded to Germany, Australia, and the UK and continued to grow and prosper while the other online ventures fell victim to the dot-com bust of 2000. In 2002, eBay purchased PayPal to secure hassle-free payments for its customers. From its humble beginnings in 1995, eBay has evolved into a household name. As of 2022, eBay is available in over 200 countries and is still among the world's biggest e-commerce platforms, with annual revenue exceeding ten billion dollars.

Upon eBay's incorporation, Pierre served as president, CEO, and chief financial officer but relinquished those positions one by one to serve as the board's chairman. In September 2020, he stepped down from eBay's board of directors while remaining the company's largest single shareholder. According to Forbes, Pierre owns about 5% of eBay and 6% of PayPal, making him one of the world's top billionaires. Pierre and his wife Pam recognized that this was far more than they and their children could ever use early on. They decided to put it to good use and created a foundation in 1999 as the first phase of their philanthropic efforts. In 2010, they joined Bill Gates and Warren Buffett's "giving pledge" to donate at least half of their wealth to charity.

Chapter 11

The Two Sides of the Church

The Story of Eventbrite's Founders

"Time is the friend of the wonderful company, the enemy of the mediocre."
—*Warren Buffett*

Eventbrite is one of the leading self-service online platforms that enable people to set up, promote, and sell out any event. Eventbrite charges a fee to event organizers in exchange for online ticketing services unless the event is free. Julia and Kevin Hartz, then newly engaged, founded Eventbrite in 2006 in San Francisco, California, while planning a wedding together.

Julia majored in television production and began a career in television in Los Angeles as an executive at MTV and then at FX networks after graduation. Around that time, she met Kevin Hartz at the wedding of her boss at MTV, who was marrying Kevin's classmate from Stanford. Half of those present at the ceremony held in the church were in media and entertainment, and the other half were Stanford University folks.

Kevin grew up in an intellectually curious family. After graduating from Stanford and getting a master's in British History from

Oxford, he followed a path of intellectual curiosity, eventually ending up in the tech industry, rolling all his savings into his friends' startup. That startup was PayPal which had quick success and was acquired by eBay for $1.5 billion in 2003. Kevin had the chance to watch how PayPal assembled a talented team and blasted off at a time when the rest of the internet companies were collapsing during the dot-com crash.

Julia met Kevin when he was building his second startup, Xoom, an international money transfer company, in San Francisco. A transformation began in Julia's life when the two met. She realized that she could actually build something and decided to make a major transition in her life. Julia and Kevin decided to start a company together and began looking for an industry they could disrupt with technology.

After some searching, Julia and Kevin felt that there hadn't been a lot of innovation in ticketing registration in 2006. It was one of the last areas of e-commerce that hadn't been appropriately addressed. They decided to build a ticketing product, called Eventbrite, that would be self-service and effectively enable anybody to gather others around a common cause. They knew that online technology could make it easier, but they weren't sure how, as it was still the early days of social media.

Soon after they got engaged, Julia and Kevin started Eventbrite with a third co-founder, Renaud Visage, who was in Paris most of the year. Renaud had been a software engineer for a photo-sharing site in Silicon Valley during the dot-com bubble. A few days after Julia packed up her window office on the 42nd floor of Fox Plaza in Beverly Hills, the newly engaged couple moved to their company's new office, a windowless room at a warehouse in San Francisco. Still, they had a lot of optimism despite their humble surroundings.

Kevin was in charge of product development and Renaud was building the website, while Julia's role at their new startup was marketing and customer service. Her job was to find their customers, talk to them daily, take their feedback, and send it to Kevin. She was also in charge of their finances, but it wasn't that hard because they were not making any money. For two years, it was just the three co-founders bootstrapping the company. Julia and Kevin got married six months after starting Eventbrite and had their first child a year later. Julia answered customer emails from the labor and delivery room when they had their first child.

Eventbrite started off as a free service based on only PayPal. It provided a basic, low-friction system in which anybody could sign up, publish an event, and start selling tickets in a matter of minutes. But they had no customers in the very beginning. They had to find their early adopter group, so they spoke to their friends and colleagues in the tech industry in San Francisco, who began using Eventbrite for organizing local events for bloggers to gather for tech meetups and conferences in Silicon Valley. When Eventbrite found more users, they started expanding to more cities and charging for their service. People in places like New York quickly adopted Eventbrite because it was self-service and easily accessible.

Kevin and Julia had spent about a quarter of a million dollars in the first two years getting Eventbrite to a breakeven status. By the end of 2008, the great recession had already started, and markets collapsed. They were terrified and didn't know what would happen with their own business, so they began to go out and raise venture capital, but everyone in Silicon Valley turned them down. After some time, they decided to just put their heads down and build their business themselves, focusing on being customer-centric instead of worrying about money. Eventbrite blossomed again in 2009 while most other companies were still struggling.

Kevin served as the Eventbrite CEO for the first ten years until stepping down in 2016 due to health issues. By then, Julia and Kevin had sat at desks next to each other for a whole decade. Julia was terrified of what would happen when they weren't working together every day. During that challenging time, Julia stepped up while taking care of Kevin and became the CEO. Julia drove Eventbrite towards its IPO, which valued the company at around two billion dollars. As of 2022, Eventbrite has turned into a global business that powers millions of events in more than 150 countries worldwide

Chapter 12

Power to The People

The Story of Expedia and Zillow's Founder

"Be excellent to each other."
—*Bill and Ted (Bill & Ted's Excellent Adventure, 1989 film)*

Nowadays, everyone has access to several websites and apps to book flights or reserve hotel rooms with the click of a button. But when Richard "Rich" Barton started Expedia in 1996, travel planning wasn't as convenient, and people had to make their reservations with the help of a travel agent. Similarly, real estate has significantly changed in recent years; people can now efficiently buy, sell, and rent properties on various online platforms. One such pioneering platform is Zillow, founded by the same man, Rich Barton, and another former Expedia employee Lloyd Frink in 2006 when searching for their next homes.

Rich graduated from Stanford University in 1989 with a general engineering degree. After a short time in consulting, he made his way to Microsoft, still a relatively small company of only about 3000 people, when he joined it. Rich became a product marketing manager of the operating system DOS 5. It was the first time that Microsoft would market an operating system upgrade, and they brought Rich in to sell upgrades to regular PC customers.

Rich had to travel often as a product manager, and he found dealing with the corporate travel agency for his business travel frustrating. His most frequent trip was from Seattle, where he was working, making a stop in Denver, then to Buffalo in New York, then to Dallas, and then back to Seattle. It was very complicated to plan with the corporate travel agent on the phone, and Rich would hear clicking on the keyboard while the agent looked at a screen and told him fares and hotels. Yet, he couldn't see the screen! The internet had recently started, but the graphical web did not exist yet. Rich knew people used online consumer services, like America Online, to access information. So, at 26 years old, while working at Microsoft, the idea of a startup occurred to him. Rich saw a real opportunity in creating a system that allowed people to book trips themselves by taking the system that the travel agents used and making it available to people.

Since Microsoft was still small, Rich had the opportunity to update Bill Gates on projects he was working on. In one of those meetings, he pitched his idea of building an electronic travel agency to Bill Gates. Since his startup idea wasn't really a software business, Rich assumed Microsoft wouldn't be interested in it. So, he asked Bill Gates for funds, like a venture capital investment, to build that startup outside of the company. Bill Gates liked Rich's idea because it would make software previously only available on mainframes in the travel industry accessible on personal computers, which would result in more Windows sales. Bill Gates said, "Start inside of Microsoft. If it works out and you want to be separated from Microsoft, we'll think about spinning it off then." And thus, Expedia was founded as a division of Microsoft in 1996.

The internet was quickly getting more popular, and Rich wanted to expedite his company's growth. He asked Microsoft for $100 million to spend on television advertising, but they declined. Bill Gates, however, honored their pledge to consider separating Expedia from Microsoft, and Rich knew that they could raise enough money from the public markets to spend on television advertising. Companies could easily go public during the first internet bubble, so Expedia became independent of Microsoft and went public in 1999, making Rich the CEO of a public company at 32 years old.

Shortly after Expedia went public, the dot-com bubble burst, and many internet companies went down with it. Expedia was not spared the crash that hit the market. But since Expedia had a real, profitable business, it kept growing and survived the crisis. Expedia was a public company for a few years until a buyer, Barry Diller, a media mogul who wanted to get out of the media industry and into the internet, came along in 2003. Diller made an offer to purchase Expedia that was too good to resist, so Expedia was sold.

After selling Expedia, Rich left the company, and he and his wife decided to take a little break. They moved to Italy with their three young children and lived in Florence for a year. Rich wanted to find his inner artist there, so he took a life drawing class and tried writing, among other things. But at 35 years old, he felt it was too early for him to retire, and startup ideas kept coming to his mind. Rich moved back to the United States from Italy and immediately began considering new business ventures.

Rich shared an office with Lloyd Frink, a friend he'd met at Stanford and his former colleague at Microsoft and Expedia upon his return from Italy. Lloyd was from Seattle and went to the same high school that the founders of Microsoft, Bill Gates and Paul Allen, did. They were nine years apart in age and didn't really know each other, but their mothers were acquainted, and Lloyd met Bill Gates at 13. When Lloyd started working there part-time, Microsoft had about 25 employees. Lloyd answered support calls and letters that none of the Microsoft employees wanted to answer for ten summers while attending school. After college, he went to work for Microsoft full-time. Later on, he was a key part of the team that built Expedia and went on to work there. Lloyd had left Expedia around the same time that Rich came back from Italy.

Rich and Lloyd decided to start a new company and started brainstorming ideas together in 2005. Coincidently, they both were shopping for homes around the same time. By then, the web had been around for a long time, so they were surprised by how little information they could find online about what homes were available for sale. They couldn't get basic marketplace information, like what a house was actually worth, its square footage, pictures of the inside, tax record, and so on. Online real estate in 2005 was similar to how online travel had been when they started Expedia. Rich and Lloyd realized that there was an opportunity to make an online real estate business and thought, "What if we take homes and put them up on the web for an auction? Wouldn't it be more efficient if people could bid for and buy a home on the internet?" After deciding to start their new company, Rich and Lloyd sought a name for their new enterprise. They came up with some ideas, but they didn't want to spend a lot on a domain. Even back then, premium URLs would go for millions of dollars. They eventually put the zillion and pillow together and came up with Zillow. Lloyd bought Zillow.com for $9.99 on GoDaddy.

Rich and Lloyd knew that one of the hardest things about selling a house was trying to figure out its price. They went to their county's website and pulled the public data of the recent sales, then they went to the MLS website and pulled the data of what homes were on the market. They tried to put them into a spreadsheet to figure out how much the homes they were looking at should be worth. By knowing the sale price per square foot and estimating the appreciation rate of that year, they could get a general idea of a home's valuation. It was simple math, but no website was doing that at the time, so they decided to do this for all homes in the country and put dollars on the map, calling their novel feature "Zestimate."

In 2006, Rich and Lloyd launched Zillow.com. Zestimate had a significant emotional appeal because people wanted to see what their homes were worth. Mass media picked it up very quickly on the day they launched; there were great articles in the Wall Street Journal and the New York Times. It drew so many people on launch day that the site went down, and it took them half a day to bring it back up. Zillow's website had over a million visits by the second day, and by the fifth, that number had gone over two million.

Zillow was growing fast, but it was still a young startup in the real estate business when the global financial crisis hit in 2008. Coincidently, that financial crisis was catalyzed by the real estate business and bad mortgages. At the time, Zillow had three to four million users per month with no revenue and about 150 employees. Zillow was still living on venture capital, and it wasn't clear if they would ever be able to survive. Their payroll was high because most of them were engineers, so as the CEO, Rich made the hard decision to lay off about a third of the company. After making that difficult choice, Rich focused on driving revenue. Those efforts paid off, and the company made it through the financial crisis. In 2011, when Zillow went public, it had about a billion dollars in revenue. A decade later, the Seattle-based company, now known as Zillow Group, is a giant in the world of real estate with more than 5000 employees and a market value above thirty billion dollars. As of 2022, Zillow is one of the world's largest real estate marketplaces and has millions of monthly unique visitors.

Rich ran Zillow for the first six years, then became the executive chairman before retaking the CEO role in 2019. During this time, he also co-founded Glassdoor.com, a popular website for company reviews and job postings, with Robert Homan, one of his friends at Expedia. As a co-founder of Expedia, Zillow, and Glassdoor, Rich has always wanted to give power to people to make their own choices. Today, the three websites Rich created are among the top options for anyone who wants to plan a trip, buy a new house, or find a new job.

Chapter 13

Little Dorm Room

The Story of Facebook's Founder

President John F. Kennedy was visiting NASA headquarters for the first time in 1961. While touring the facility, he introduced himself to a janitor mopping the floor and asked him what he did at NASA. The janitor said, "I'm helping put a man on the moon."

Everyone knows about Facebook; it is the largest online social network in the world. Facebook was launched by Mark Zuckerberg in February 2004 as a student directory for Harvard University students, but today has more than two billion users worldwide.

Mark Zuckerberg was born in 1984. He grew up in Dobbs Ferry, north of New York City. When Mark was about ten years old, he taught himself the computer language C++, and by ninth grade, he had created a digital board game. Mark also created many programs like chat systems and a music player throughout his childhood to amuse himself.

When Mark grew bored at his local high school, he decided to go to Exeter Academy, a renowned and highly selective boarding school, where he and his friend Adam D'Angelo created a music website called "Synapse," which could determine a user's music listening preferences. The website became so popular that Microsoft and other big tech companies wanted to buy it for over a million dollars and recruit Mark right out of Exeter. Yet, Mark turned them down and instead enrolled in Harvard University in 2002.

Mark had found Latin and Greek fascinating in high school, so he planned to major in the classics. However, once at Harvard, he became more and more interested in psychology after interacting with many people and finally switched to a psychology major. But he retained his love of computers and took more computer science classes in college than psychology classes. Mark was trying to figure out what classes to take in the fall semester of sophomore year and was curious about what his friends were planning to take and had taken in the past, but there was no database to give him that information. So he wrote a code that scraped the course catalog and let people input what classes they wanted, which he launched as a website called Course-Match. Mark ran his website from his laptop in his dorm room. Unfortunately, his desk was next to the bathroom, where steam always poured out when people were showering, which fried Mark's laptop, causing him to lose all his website's data after a few weeks of running it.

Mark got himself in trouble with the next website he built in college. He hacked into the school's computers to collect students' images and created a prank website called FaceMash, which listed Harvard students and ranked them by hotness. FaceMash became a campus sensation, but it also upset many people who felt mocked and exposed by it. Mark shut down the site under pressure when the Harvard administration board charged him with breaching security and violating individual privacy. Everyone thought that Mark would get kicked out of school and didn't wait for the board to make their final decision. His parents came to help him pack, and his friends threw him a "going-away party." Mark met his future wife, Priscilla Chan, at that party while they were in line for the bathroom. Mark said, "I'm going to get kicked out in three days, so we need to go on a date right away." Priscilla and Mark started dating, but Harvard didn't expel Mark in the end.

The experience of CourseMatch and FaceMash got Mark thinking about channeling a community's energy to build some kind of shared asset. Around the same time, Facemash got the attention of three Harvard upperclassmen students: Olympic rowers and twins, Cameron and Tyler Winklevoss, and their partner, Divya Narendra. They had been trying to build a social network site called Harvard Connection for more than a year. Two of their original programmers had left the team, and none of those remaining were computer programmers, so they needed someone to write the hard lines of code. They thought Mark was the person they were looking for and reached out to him. Mark found their idea exciting, but instead of working on Harvard Connection, he began working on a similar social networking website based on the Harvard student directory called Facebook, which later sparked a furious battle over how Facebook was actually created.

Harvard had a "study period" before final exams in January. During that time, students would typically study for their finals, but Mark used that period to write the first version of Facebook. One of Mark's courses was called "Rome of Augustus," which focused on art history. On the final day, students were asked to write an essay about the historical significance of specific pieces of art. Mark hadn't really gone to class all term, and he had been programming Facebook during the reading period. To pass the final, he went to the course website, downloaded all the images, and made a simple page website that would randomly show the images and let people contribute what they thought was significant about them. He emailed the website to the class list and said, "Hey guys, I built a study tool for anyone that finds this interesting." Within an hour, the whole website was populated with all the information needed for the final. After the final exam, the professor mentioned that they were the highest final grades he had ever seen.

Mark partnered with Eduardo Saverin, his classmate at Harvard, to fund Facebook. Eduardo put up a thousand dollars to launch the site, and in February of 2004, Mark launched Facebook from his little dorm room. That night, he went to the cafe with his friends and told them, "I am excited to connect the Harvard community, but one day someone will connect the whole world." In the beginning, Facebook was very simple. Users could look people up, see profiles, and poke others, but there were no messages, and all the other elements were built over time. Still, Facebook quickly became very popular at Harvard, and of the 5,000 undergrads at Harvard, three-quarters of them had signed up on Facebook within the first two weeks.

The Winklevoss brothers and Divya Narendra found out about Facebook the same way nearly everyone else at Harvard did. A few days after Mark launched the site, the Winklevoss twins and Divya Narendra sent Mark a cease-and-desist letter, accusing Mark of violating their contract. Mark responded with a letter denying any wrongdoing, claiming his site was a separate venture and used none of the same code. The Winklevoss twins and Narendra would later appeal a settlement with Facebook, but they lost in a federal court.

Facebook had incredible momentum at Harvard from the beginning, so Mark and his friends thought it would work at other schools too, and soon they launched it at Columbia, Yale, and Stanford. They chose those three schools because they all had some sort of preexisting online community, and they wanted to see how Facebook competed with those school-specific social networks. Within a couple of weeks, Facebook had thousands of users in each of those three schools. After that successful experience, they decided to go all out; they launched Facebook college by college while optimizing the platform and offering new features. As soon as Facebook opened up at a school, most students would be on it within weeks, and by the end of the year, Facebook was in twenty-nine schools. When they saw Facebook take off at those schools, they realized that it could be worth putting their time into it.

Mark tried to avoid spending a lot from the very beginning as he had no plan to raise money. Facebook's first server cost them $85, which was the gating factor for them to launch in new schools. To afford more servers, they started putting ads on the site. Eduardo was responsible for finding more ads and ensuring that they had enough money to keep things running, while Mark worked on efficiency, trying to fit more schools onto each server. After some time, they started meeting with bigger advertisers and some venture capitalists. Mark and Eduardo had dinner with Sean Parker, the 24-year-old co-founder of the file-sharing website Napster, on a trip to New York. Sean believed that Facebook was a brilliant idea that could be worth billions of dollars, but Eduardo was skeptical and didn't think they needed Sean's help.

Mark visited a couple of his friends during the spring break, one of whom was at Stanford in Palo Alto, California. He had never been to California before. After arriving at San Francisco airport and driving down the highway to Palo Alto, he saw all the buildings of the technology companies and thought, "This is amazing. It's where all these technology startups come from." When his sophomore summer came around, Mark and his friends who worked on Facebook decided to spend some time off-campus, so they rented a house in Palo Alto to be around other great technology companies.

Once they came to California, Mark reconnected with Sean Parker, who lived in the Bay Area and later became his roommate. Sean showed Mark how things were done in Silicon Valley, including how to meet investors and negotiate with them and who to hire. After some time, Sean Parker became the new president of Facebook and introduced Mark to Peter Thiel, one of PayPal's co-founders. Mark told him their plan, and Peter Thiel invested five hundred thousand dollars in the company. But when Mark explained they planned on going back to school, Peter demanded that all the founders be on vesting schedules, which Mark hadn't heard of before. When Mark and Eduardo started the company together at Harvard, they divided the equity. But Eduardo never moved out to California with the rest of the Facebook team and remained on the East Coast, and as Sean got more involved with Facebook, things became tense between Mark and Eduardo. Meanwhile, Facebook was growing astronomically fast. While Eduardo was supposed to be the company's business head, Mark and Sean were taking meetings with venture capitalists all over

California. So they eventually decided to run the business without Eduardo and removed him.

When Mark and his friends came to Palo Alto for summer, they had not considered moving to California or dropping out of Harvard. But one day, one of Mark's friends said, "We have a lot of users, and we are getting an increasing number of servers, but we have no dedicated operations expert and have to manage our own servers. I don't think we can do this and take a full course load, so why don't we just take one term off to build what we need to run Facebook more autonomously? We can go back for the spring semester." Harvard had a policy that let students take as much time as they wanted off school, so Mark and his friends took the fall semester off. When the spring term came along, they hadn't quite built the automation process, so they decided to take another hiatus. After taking several terms off, they realized they would have to stay in California and finally dropped out of Harvard.

Facebook had millions of users across more than one thousand university campuses nationwide within one year. By then, big money had started pouring in, and several venture capital firms wanted to invest millions into the site. Mark opened Facebook to the general public in 2006; the response was stunning. Around the same time, Mark made a change that gave Facebook a sudden and dramatic boost. Facebook allowed people to identify or tag themselves and their friends in photos. That huge innovation led to a massive increase in users at Facebook; membership doubled, with images becoming the biggest driving growth factor.

Then big companies began showing interest in buying Facebook. Yahoo baited the 22-year-old Mark with an extraordinary offer; a buyout for one billion dollars. But Mark didn't want to sell because he hoped to expand Facebook to see if he could connect with more people. Facebook was building the first News Feed at the time, and he thought launching News Feed could change how people learn about the world. However, nearly everyone else at Facebook wanted to sell the company to Yahoo. After one tense argument, an advisor told him if he didn't agree to sell, he would regret the decision for the rest of his life. Still, Mark refused the offer, and every person on the management team was gone within a year. That was a challenging time for Mark to lead Facebook as he felt alone, but he stayed faithful to his mission.

In 2007, Microsoft offered Mark a deal he couldn't turn down. Microsoft paid $250 million for 1.6 percent of the company, valuing Facebook at $15 billion. Suddenly everyone was talking about Facebook and its deal with Microsoft. In April 2012, Facebook paid one billion dollars to acquire the popular photo-sharing platform Instagram. One month later, it went public in the largest IPO on record for an internet company, making Mark a multi-billionaire.

Today, Mark's platform, created at the age of 19, is the world's largest online social network with over 2 billion monthly active users. Over the years, Facebook acquired other successful startups like WhatsApp and Oculus, which produces virtual reality headsets. To reflect on its vast range of products and emphasize its focus on metaverse, Facebook rebranded the company and changed its name to Meta Platforms, widely known as Meta, in late 2021. As of early 2022, Meta's 37-year-old CEO has an estimated net worth of more than 100 billion dollars, making him one of the world's top ten richest people. But Mark doesn't want to use that wealth for himself; he and his wife Priscilla have pledged to donate 99% of their Facebook stake to charitable causes over their lifetimes.

Chapter 14

From the Vietnam War to Computer Hobbyist

The Story of GoDaddy's Founder

"The temptation to quit will be greatest just before you are about to succeed."
—*Chinese Proverb*

Making one's own website is very easy these days. GoDaddy is one of the world's largest domain registrars. Although the premium domain names, if you find any, could value millions of dollars, some of the regular domains can be purchased at Godaddy.com for as low as $2.99 for a year. They also provide web hosting and a wide range of other services like website builders and e-commerce solutions. GoDaddy was founded in 1999 in Arizona by Bob Parsons.

Bob Parsons was born in 1950 in Baltimore, Maryland. He wasn't an excellent student from elementary through high school. When Bob was a little kid, his dad found religion and became a Catholic. At that time, Bob was in the third grade and went to a public school in Baltimore until, like his dad, Bob became Catholic and transferred to St. Elizabeth of Hungary Catholic school. Initially, he didn't do well in his new school except in math because he had no religious education previously. Still, he managed to pass the third and fourth grades.

On the last day of fifth grade, Bob was waiting for his teacher, Sister Brenda, to hand out report cards. He knew he had not passed when Sister Brenda gave everyone their report cards except Bob and two other classmates. She told everybody except those three to get in line and told Bob and the other two students, "You guys stay here until I come back." Every year on the last day of school, Bob's father picked him and his brother up from school, and they would show him their report cards. His dad was a pretty hard, blue-collar guy, so Bob thought there was no way he could tell his father that he had failed. So Bob got in line with the rest of the class without his teacher noticing and followed them out. Bob went to the waiting parents with the rest of his class and saw his father waiting with his little brother. His father asked, "Where is your report card?" Bob replied, "They didn't give me one." His father told them to get in the car and brought them to a sporting goods store where every year he bought them a little something for graduating. His father said, "Bob, don't you want anything?" He said, "No, dad, I'm good." When they got home, his brother ran and gave his report card to their mother. She asked, "Where's your report card, Bob?" He again responded, "I don't have one. The teacher didn't give it to me." His mother said, "I've never heard that. I'm going to call your teacher," but she never called, nor did the school.

Bob and his brother went to the school when classes began again, but Bob didn't know what would happen. There were separate lines for each class, and Bob got into the sixth grader's line. But as the lines started going to their classrooms, the teacher grabbed him and said, "Sister Brenda told me what you did. She told me you failed, but you didn't wait for her to talk to you. She didn't know what to do, so she passed you!" Bob instantly realized that taking risks and putting ideas into action wasn't that bad! He managed to pass the sixth grade and came home with the report card. His mother said to him, "Your grades aren't great, but I like it better when you receive a report card."

Bob wasn't the best student in high school either and struggled to pass. When he was 17, with graduation looming in April, he was failing every subject except gym. A couple of his friends approached him at the gym and said, "Bob, what are you going to do after school? We are going down to see a Marine Corps recruiter. Why don't you come with us?" So, Bob ended up joining the Marine Corps, and his high school teachers passed him once he enlisted.

After joining the Marine Corps, Bob first went to a boot camp, and then in 1968, he was sent to the raging war in Vietnam, where he became a combat rifleman. When he first got to his unit in Vietnam, he was one of the replacements for four soldiers killed two days before his arrival. The longest time anyone in his squad had survived was six weeks. Bob didn't think he had a chance of getting out of there alive. He accepted that he would die there and made his goal just to make it through each day. After a month and a half, Bob was wounded and taken to a hospital in Japan, where he stayed for two months. After the hospital, he went back to Vietnam but never returned to combat again. His experience at Marine Corps taught him discipline, commitment, and responsibility.

Bob came back home and got a difficult job at a steel mill, where he worked there for a few years until he decided to go to college. He went to the University of Baltimore and studied accounting. Bob's academic performance turned around in college, and he graduated magna cum laude. Even though it was one of the few courses he didn't get an A in, Introduction to Data Processing was one of his favorite classes. Bob took the CPA exam after graduation and passed it the first time.

Bob became an accountant and started working for a medical publisher in Baltimore. Five years later, he became an accountant at the Commercial Credit Leasing Court, which had a division that leased automobiles and sent their accountants out to companies they wanted to acquire to review their records and provide a spreadsheet listing all the leases. They sent Bob to Redwood City in California to look at an automobile leasing company for one of those projects. Bob finished up early and had twelve hours left before his flight. Since he liked bookstores and Redwood City was close to the Stanford University campus, he went to the Stanford bookstore, where he found a book about programming a basic computer language, which seemed interesting. So Bob bought the book and started reading it at the airport while waiting for his flight.

On the flight back home, Bob got an idea to write a program to analyze the leases he was looking at for his employer. He learned the basics of coding from the book he bought on that flight, and when he was back, he started programming the computer in his employer's office. It took him a couple of weeks to get it working, but from then on, Bob would write a code any time there was a problem he needed to decipher. After some time, he bought an Apple 2 computer and started programming on that, which he enjoyed. He became a computer hobbyist who never bought any software; he wrote the code himself if he wanted the computer to do something. Bob kept learning different programming languages and got to the point where he was pretty good at coding. Then, in 1984, Bob wrote a program that analyzed his personal accounting and money management, like balancing the checkbook, budgeting, and providing financial statements and graphics. He called his software MoneyCounts and decided to try selling it since he had been working on it for several years and was sure his software was good. He created a little business in his basement, calling it "Parsons Technology."

Bob put his software for sale for $129, but no one bought it. He tried everything, even different packaging, but nothing worked, and he lost his $15,000 in savings within the first year. Later, Bob reduced the price to $89 and then $69, but his sales were still poor. He managed to scrape together $25,000 from his tax return, credit cards, and a bonus from his job, but he lost it in his second year of business. Finally, a break came in the third year when Bob was almost broke. A company that sold advertising on the front page of a computer magazine called him. They normally sold the ad on the magazine's front page for $15000, but the company supposed to buy it had folded, so they gave Bob a deal to buy it for $4000. He got the ad and then dropped the price of his software all the way to $12. Software back then was protected by copyright laws, but he noted on his ad that the buyers could copy it or give it away to someone. The ad took off, and many people bought the software.

In 1987, Bob quit his job and started working on his company full-time. He built it up to the point it had a thousand employees and $100 million in assets. After running Parsons Technology for ten years, Bob sold it to Intuit in 1994 for $64 million. As the only investor, all of the money came to Bob, and he remained the company's chairman until a year later when he decided to retire. After getting divorced from his wife and splitting the money with her, he moved to Arizona. But Bob soon realized he hated retirement and wanted to get back into the business, but he wasn't sure what to do after a year of not working. However, he had learned from his last company that he needed to be involved with something to see the opportunities. The dot-com boom was just starting in 1997, so Bob hired about thirty people and started trying different things on the internet, from education to building a network and selling software, but none of them worked.

Back then, it was difficult and expensive to build a website, so Bob decided to simplify that process and developed Website Complete, a do-it-yourself package. Unfortunately, he sold very little software after its launch. Then Bob realized that every website needed a domain name, but all the major domain registrars at the time sucked because their prices were high, and they didn't have any customer support. So, Bob decided to start a domain registrar in 1999, when the internet was still booming. Bob knew that it would take at least a year to build the software and the required infrastructure, and he had to post about $1 million in bonds. It was a big commitment, but he decided to do it anyway and called his new company GoDaddy. By the time GoDaddy was ready, the internet bubble was about to burst, and Bob's company sold its first domain name in November 2000, amid the dot-com crash.

Back then, all internet companies were judged by cash burn. Bob had about $32 million when he started, but the company hemorrhaged funds over time, losing one to two million dollars a month. By early 2001, only $6 million were left, which seemed like it would become zero very soon. At that point, Bob decided he would have to sell the company. Bob wanted to get away to think things through for a week, so he flew to Hawaii without telling anybody about his decision. But once there, he realized that the money didn't mean anything to him, and he really wanted to keep the company going. Bob thought, "If my company fails, I can still do another job happily. Some of the happiest times in my life were when I was poor." He came back determined not to give up. About seven months later, GoDaddy turned around and survived the dot-com crash. By October 2001, GoDaddy became profitable and was one of the few companies paying its bills, while its competitors vanished by the dozen every week.

GoDaddy continued rapidly expanding until it had a 16% market share worldwide in 2005. To increase that, Bob decided to run a Superbowl ad. However, Fox network canceled their ad at the last minute. As a result, all the media picked up the news that an ad was canceled after being approved for Superbowl for the first time ever. The ad was repeatedly shown on all the media, from news channels to radio shows and newspapers, generating free publicity. Because of that canceled ad, GoDaddy's worldwide market share jumped from 16% to 25% in a week. As of early 2022, GoDaddy still has the largest global market share in domain registration and web hosting.

In 2011, Bob Parsons resigned from his position as CEO of GoDaddy and sold approximately 70 percent of his company to a private equity firm. In 2014, he stepped down from his Executive Chairman position and served on the board until 2018, when he sold off his remaining stake in the web hosting firm. Bob's entrepreneurial journey, however, did not end there. The billionaire now owns shopping malls, motorcycle dealerships, and a golf club and has invested hundreds of millions of dollars in real estate in Arizona, where he now lives. Bob and his wife are also active philanthropists and have joined Bill Gates and Warren Buffett's pledge to donate at least half of their fortunes to charity.

Chapter 15

In the Middle of the Night

The Story of Google's Founders

"The present is theirs; the future, for which I really worked, is mine."
—Nicola Tesla

Google needs no introduction. The most popular search engine on the internet helps people find the answer to most of their questions, from how to apply college to recipes for making cookies. "Googling" has even become a verb synonymous with "searching" for information. Google was started as a research project at Stanford University by two graduate students, Larry Page and Sergey Brin, in 1996.

Larry Page was born in 1973 in Michigan. His parents met in 1962 at the University of Michigan, where they both studied and got advanced degrees in computer science, which was unusual at that time because this was still a developing field in the 60s. Having a computer in 1978 was pretty uncommon, but because Larry's father was a computer science professor, they had one in their house when Larry was six. Larry amazed his teachers in his elementary school when he turned in a word-processed assignment.

Growing up, Larry always wanted to be an inventor. When he was twelve, his parents gave him an autobiography of Nichola Tesla. To Larry, Tesla seemed like the greatest inventor that he could imagine; he was the person who invented AC power, generators, and all sorts of other things. Yet, Larry cried once he finished reading the story of Tesla's life because he realized someone could be the world's greatest inventor and still be a failure if he had trouble funding his inventions. Larry believed Tesla would have been able to do more if he was better at commercializing his projects and thought, "I don't want to be like Tesla. I want to invent things and make sure they get out in the world and make a real impact." Larry's idea was to start a company or become a professor to support his projects.

Some years later, Larry began attending the same school as his parents, the University of Michigan, to study computer engineering. In college, Larry participated in a training program called Leader-Shape. Their slogan was "have a healthy disregard for the impossible." That program encouraged him to pursue a crazy idea to build a rapid transit system on campus to replace the buses. He wanted to create a monorail between the central and north campuses. It was only a two-mile trip, but forty diesel buses ran back and forth over that distance. Larry's idea of that transit system was a futuristic way of solving the transportation problem, but ultimately, it never became a reality. Still, he always kept his interest in transportation and sustainable energy.

In 1995, Larry moved to Stanford for grad school, where he met Sergey Brin, a computer science PhD student studying data mining, a field for analyzing large amounts of data to discover their patterns and trends. Sergey was born in the Soviet Union in 1973 to Jewish parents who were mathematicians. Sergey's parents had limited career opportunities in their home country, so they came to the US when he was six. Sergey was always interested in mathematics and enjoyed doing math problems as a kid. He had also always been interested in computers ever since he got one in elementary school. Sergey made little programs in middle school that could talk back to people using artificial intelligence. He did his undergrad in math and computer science and then joined the PhD program of computer science at

Stanford. Larry and Sergey didn't like each other very much initially, and they debated every point. Larry would comment on every single thing and was combative in every conversation. But they eventually grew to become good friends.

Larry had several different ideas for his PhD project, but his advisor said, "Why don't you focus on the web for a while?" That was excellent advice because the web was growing very rapidly in 1995, but it still had a lot of unknowns and potential. As Larry was looking for a research idea related to the web, one night, he woke up in the middle of the night after having a vivid dream. His dream was, "I could download the entire web onto some old computers that are lying around." He found a pencil and pad by his bed and started taking notes before his dream was lost, then he stayed up a couple of hours to do some math. He realized his dream was pretty plausible, assuming to keep only the web links, not any pages. At the time, the web was just five years old with less than twenty-five thousand websites, and based on his calculations, Larry thought it would take a couple of weeks to download the whole web.

The next day, Larry told his advisor about his idea of downloading the web and how long he thought it would take. His advisor nodded and didn't discourage Larry by telling him he suspected it would take much longer. Neither of them knew exactly what he would do with the web links, but it seemed like something no one else was looking at. So, they decided that would be a good thing to research. Larry hoped he could get a dissertation with that research and do something fun and perhaps also practical at the same time.

Larry started collecting the web links in late 1995, but it took him more than a year to finish. The downloaded web was interesting data for mining, so Larry asked his friend Sergey to look at the data he had gathered. Sergey became interested in making sense of all the pages on the internet and finding their patterns. After spending some time, Larry and Sergey noticed that there were hundreds or even thousands of other pages behind every web page that linked to it. They started to record each page's backlinks and realized that websites with more backlinks pointing to them were normally more reputable than those with fewer. They figured that their list of backlinks could be used for ranking search results more accurately than the existing methods at the time. In the 90s, searching the internet was very slow and rudimentary, often returning completely useless results; for example, if someone typed Stanford, they would get random pages that mentioned Stanford. Users would often have to sift through pages of links to find a relevant website because search engines couldn't really understand which pages were more important.

Larry and Sergey called their invented algorithm for ranking weblinks PageRank. In the beginning, they never considered building their own search engine. Their plan was to sell their technology, so they started talking to the people in the industry who were working on searches. They met with a handful of companies, including Excite and Yahoo, two of the biggest brands in search at the time. Excite came very close to buying PageRank for a mere one million dollars, but eventually, it backed out of the deal. Larry and Sergey then met with Yahoo co-founders David Filo and Jerry Yang. They were impressed with their invention, but it seemed to work too well for them. Yahoo's business model at the time centered around being a destination, so they generated more money the longer users were on their platform. Having a better search engine would hurt this model. David Filo told them, "This is a great search technology. Why don't you guys make a company, and maybe we'll use you someday?" Larry and Sergey realized that nobody in the industry was really interested in improving their search engines, so they decided to make their own instead of selling their invention.

PageRank could make the ultimate search engine to understand what someone wanted and give them the right thing using artificial intelligence. But Larry and Sergey were worried about dropping out of their PhD program. So, they decided to release the first version of their search engine, called BackRub, on the Stanford website. BackRub took almost half of the university's bandwidth, and they constantly needed more and more of Stanford's resources. Larry and Sergey turned to a Stanford professor for help, who introduced them to an angel investor well-connected in the tech industry. But raising money wasn't easy, and investors were skeptical. There were five search engines at the time, and everyone believed that there was no market for another one. But Larry and Sergey still wanted to organize the world's information and make it universally accessible. So finally, they decided to launch their search engine outside of Stanford for public use and changed its name to Google. Google originated from a misspelling of the word "googol," meaning a number that has a one with a hundred zeros after it. They picked that name to signify that their search engine intended to provide large amounts of information.

One day, when Larry and Sergey met with their professor at Stanford, one of his friends, a successful entrepreneur in Silicon Valley, showed up. Larry and Sergey chatted with him about their search engine and showed him a quick demo. He said, "This is fantastic. I'd be interested in investing, and I don't want you guys to worry too much about money right now. Why don't I just write you a check?" He went back to his car and came back with his checkbook, then wrote a check on the spot for $100 thousand made out to Google. Larry and Sergey had not registered a company yet and couldn't cash the check, so they registered Google as a website on September 15, 1997.

That $100 thousand helped Larry and Sergey start their company, but they still needed much more cash to buy hard disks and servers. They dropped out of their PhD programs to raise funding for their young company. However, this turned out to be no easy task because Google didn't fit into the conventional wisdom of what a website should do: keep users from migrating to another page. Finally, they found three other angel investors, including Jeff Bezos of Amazon, who gave them $1 million to get Google off the ground. Larry and Sergey incorporated Google and moved into their first office, a car garage. Google soon attracted the attention of two well-known Silicon Valley venture capitalists and raised a VC round in 1999. With the new funding, Larry and Sergey started hiring first-rate engineers, people who would meet their exacting standards. They did not launch any marketing campaign and let Google expand by word of mouth.

Larry and Sergey had created a new search engine but had yet to find a way to turn it into a profitable endeavor. The search engines back then would show sponsored pages like regular search results. However, they didn't like the idea of using advertising to cash in. Unlike rivals Yahoo and AOL, Google's homepage was famously sparse. Larry and Sergey didn't want users to see results because someone had paid for them, so to build user trust, they refused to clutter their homepage with ads. Yet, no ads at all meant no revenue. Larry and Sergey invented a new way of targeting text ads triggered by search requests; instead of distracting pop-ups or flashing ads, they placed small ads above the page, next to search results, calling it Google AdWords. It was a revolutionary idea back then that enabled big and small businesses to take control of their advertising dollars by purchasing certain keywords. Google exploded with a massive new revenue source.

By September of 2000, Google had indexed a billion URLs and was available in 15 languages. In 2001, Google brought Eric Schmidt to take over the CEO role. Larry became President of Products and Sergey became the President of Technology; the two founders still shared an office. Google kept up its spectacular growth while its rivals slowly faded away. In August of 2004, Google became a public company via an IPO, making it worth more than $23 billion, and its two founders became billionaires.

Larry and Sergey quickly moved beyond the first technology they developed at Stanford. Google bought Android in 2005 when it was a small company, and within a few years, Android had become the largest shipping smartphone operating system worldwide. The company also expanded with Google Maps, Google News, and Google Earth. In 2006, Google acquired the video-sharing website YouTube for $1.65 billion. As of 2022, Google Search and YouTube are the first and second most-visited websites on the internet.

In January 2011, Larry Page took over the CEO role again while Sergey Brin focused on new products. By then, Google had grown from a startup to a technology giant hitting billions of dollars in revenue. In August of 2015, Larry announced that Google would restructure into several subsidiaries of a new holding company known as Alphabet, with him becoming CEO of Alphabet and Sergey Brin assuming the position of its president. As Alphabet CEO, Larry got the chance to follow some of his other interests, including transportation and sustainable energy. The two Google founders stepped down from their positions at Alphabet in 2019.

Chapter 16

The Tipping Point

The Story of Groupon's Founder

"That is the paradox of the epidemic: that in order to create one contagious movement, you often have to create many small movements first."
—*Malcolm Gladwell*

Groupon is a daily-deals website and app that saves users money through virtual coupons. Much like a physical coupon book, people can use Groupon to get bargains on all sorts of things, from food and retail products to travel and services. It was founded by Andrew Mason in Chicago in 2008.

When Andrew was a graduate student studying public policy at the University of Chicago, he got the idea to make a website called "The Point." It started off when he was frustrated because he had to pay an early termination fee to a cellphone company. He realized that almost everybody had the same problem and wished there was a way to come together and refuse to pay the fee because the company couldn't charge them if no one was willing to pay. As he thought more, it became clear that this concept could apply to everything, from organizing a small group of people that buy something to boycotting multinational corporations.

Andrew developed the idea of a social platform that would allow people to either take some kind of collective action or contribute money towards something. But what was unique about The Point was that the action would happen only once the campaign hit a tipping point of participation. It was conditional on a certain number of people joining or a certain amount of money being raised, and nobody's credit card would be charged until they hit that goal. If someone was doing a boycott, they had to wait until enough people committed to the action instead of immediately starting the boycott. Then, The Point would fulfill their commitment and let everybody know that their efforts had been worthwhile.

Andrew was a program developer before he went to grad school. One of his old colleagues heard about his idea through a mutual acquaintance. He called Andrew up one day and said, "Can you come to my office and pitch your idea to me?" So, Andrew presented his idea to his former colleague, who called him back a week later and said, "I want to give you a million dollars to drop out of school and work on your idea!" Andrew didn't know anything about starting a tech company, but he decided to take the challenge anyway.

They started working on The Point at the beginning of 2006 and launched the website in September. After the launch, they had about a thousand visitors to the website every day for a while. They had some campaigns around social issues on The Point, so Andrew thought people would join those campaigns, become users, spread the word, and join other campaigns. One particular campaign to legalize weed got a lot of subscribers, and a whole community of people really rallied around that issue. Still, instead of infusing the website with positivity, they would go to all other campaigns and just troll everybody joining them, which became an awful situation.

Andrew and his partners raised another five million dollars after launching The Point, but they still struggled to grow their business. They tried everything they could think of, yet it was clear that The Point wasn't working after a year. Their investors started to hint that they wanted to take their money back. So Andrew began thinking about how to pivot to something else. He noticed that people had tried to use The Point platform for group purchasing campaigns; a group of people would get together to negotiate with a local business to get a discount. Andrew thought, "Why don't we just go out and do that ourselves?"

Andrew wanted to use the technology they had developed for The Point but had difficulty getting the rest of the team excited about doing this little coupon side project. So he decided to use his own coding skills and built a custom WordPress template for the new website himself. He then bought getyourgroupon.com because they could not afford to buy groupon.com at the time. Andrew and some of his teammates launched their new website in Chicago in late 2008 while still running The Point at the same time. It took less than a month from coming up with the idea to its actual implementation.

Andrew made a platform for collective purchasing, but they didn't have any customers or inventory of things to sell. Andrew and his team decided to start in Chicago because they could go to local businesses and convince them to sign up. The first Groupon deal was from a bar, which also sold pizza, on their building's ground floor. They negotiated a two-for-one pizza deal with the bar, which became popular. They kept adding one deal a day and collecting feedback from the merchants and customers and soon realized they were doing far better with Groupon than they ever had with The Point. It slowly became more acceptable for everyone in the company to spend their time and money on Groupon.

Groupon exceeded everyone's expectations. After a couple of months, it became the fastest-growing company in history. To avoid competition, they intentionally tried to keep it low profile. Yet, many people tried to copy Groupon, making it one of the most copied websites ever, with many versions popping worldwide. In the summer of 2009, they started to expand Groupon and launched in San Francisco. Instead of focusing on consumer goods, they focused on local products and businesses where they actually could go out and cut deals.

Groupon hit a 1-billion-dollar valuation in just 16 months, and soon, big companies wanted to acquire it. Yahoo approached Groupon and offered to buy them for around $2 billion. Andrew did not want to sell to Yahoo, but the company's board was interested in the offer. So, Andrew managed to get a meeting with Google, thinking that Google would be a better place to be part of. The negotiation with Google was going well, while Groupon's business was taking off to a new level as they were getting into the holiday season. The board looked at the new revenue numbers and decided Groupon was worth more independently and that it would be unwise to sell the company at that time. Groupon had a successful IPO in 2011, ending its first day on the market with a valuation of more than $16 billion. At the time, it was the second-biggest tech IPO in history, just behind Google's in 2004. Since then, however, the company's stock price has declined. As of early 2022, Groupon's market cap has settled just below $1 billion.

Andrew left Groupon at the beginning of 2013 and moved out to San Francisco from Chicago. He started working on a new startup called Detour; a mobile app that took people on audio-guided walks through cities. The response to the product was good, but it was hard to keep it as a standalone company. Detour ultimately failed, but once again, Andrew Mason found a clue for a new company in what was not working. In 2017, he founded Descript, a word processor for audio, which has raised tens of millions of dollars to build tools for editing audio and video files using artificial intelligence.

Chapter 17

Coloring Competition

The Story of IMDb's Founder

"Whatever you do, do it well."
—*Walt Disney*

IMDb, or The Internet Movie Database, is the largest and most comprehensive movie database on the web, which includes movies, TV shows, and cast information. IMDb, now owned by Amazon.com, was initially launched as fan-operated software and website by Colin "Col" Needham in 1990 in the UK.

One day, when five-year-old Col was staying at his grandmother's house, she said to him, "Would you like to enter a coloring competition? You could win a prize." The competition was to color a scene from Walt Disney's "Snow White and the Seven Dwarfs" in the local newspaper, and the prize was two tickets to go and see that film at the theater. Col entered the competition and won and fell in love with cinema after seeing Snow White. Besides his passion for movies, Col became very interested in technology from early on. In 1979, when he was 12 years old, he got his first home computer as a Christmas present. The computer was a build-it-yourself kit and came with the chips on a circuit board. He had to solder the chips onto the board before starting to program it. The computer had a calculator display and minimal memory but was still enough to spark his interest.

The home video revolution was taking off at the same time; video tapes (VHS) were everywhere. In the early 1980s, Col saw so many movies that he started losing track of which ones he had seen and which ones he hadn't. So, he got a paper diary and wrote down the date he saw a movie. After doing that for two weeks, he thought, "Why don't I create a database of everything that I've seen?" He then started to put his film diary in his little database; after seeing a film, he would type in the director, the main cast, the producers, etc. He could then get a report from his database that said, for example, how many Alfred Hitchcock movies he had seen. His mother would sometimes come into his bedroom and say, "Why don't you go outside and play?" Col would answer, "I'm just adding a new movie to my database." He was so obsessed with movies that he even took his little notepad to movie theaters to write down notes about them and later enter them into his database.

Col started using the internet technology very early and got his first email address in 1985. He then began to interact online with other film fans around the world and joined a film discussion group for fans of movies and TV shows. They talked about films they had seen and exchanged thoughts and impressions. Most of the people in that group were American male college students who mostly liked to talk about attractive actresses and which movies they had appeared in. One of the people in the group finally started a list of frequently asked questions about actresses and the films in which they played. Col grabbed a copy of that list and imported it into a separate table within his database, then made a list of all the actresses in all the movies he had seen. His database included records of actors, cinematographers, directors, writers, producers, etc. So Col made a list of actors and then published it online for the fan group.

Shortly after launching the actors' list, somebody emailed Col and said, "I'm a big fan of directors, and I think you should publish a director's list." Col was busy with actors, so he replied to that person and said, "Why don't you join our small team and volunteer to make the directors' file? I'll give you a list of the directors of all the films that I've seen and provide you some software to manage the data. The software will publish a new version of the list. You can email me back that new list." The guy said, "OK, I'm in." About a month later, another person in the group said, "These lists are great, but we need a database that we can search." Col decided to build that and published the first version of the IMDb software, called rec.arts.movies database at the time, in October of 1990. The software allowed people to download the files onto their own computers and had a command-line interface for basic searches, which people could use to search for things like who directed a set of movies.

The new requests kept coming; a couple of weeks later, Col received another email that asked for writers, so Col and his volunteer team added a writer section. Then someone emailed him about composers. That person had his own composers' record because he collected soundtrack CDs, so he helped Col create the composer database. Every now and then, somebody would pop up and ask for something else. Driven by those requests, they slowly started launching new lists; the genres list began with two genres, the quotes list started with five movie quotes, the biography list with two biographies, and so on. As soon as they launched them, the community responded and contributed. The data was pouring in, and by the end of 1990, they had 10,000 movies in their database.

When Col started developing his movie database software, there was no World Wide Web or commercial use of the internet. But in the summer of 1993, Col got an email from a PhD computer science student at Cardiff University in Wales who said, "Hi Col, I just installed the movie database software, and I think it's terrific. Have you heard of this World Wide Web thing? I think it might become quite big, and I would love to write a wrapper around the software, and we could do the website interface." Col had heard of the World Wide Web, so he went to Cardiff University and spoke to that PhD student and the professors. The computer science department said that Col could use the spare capacity of Cardiff University servers for his project.

A few weeks later, the PhD student emailed Col and said their website was launched on the university server. It had tens of hits within one hour, and for the first time, Col and his team got real-time feedback from people using their movie database. Soon, their website filled up all the space of Cardiff University's servers. Col put a note on the bottom of their website asking if other universities would like to host a copy of their database. They got many answers back, and soon, their website data was on the servers in the US, Germany, South Korea, Japan, Italy, Australia, and Iceland. They kept running their website on the universities' servers for a couple of years while it was constantly growing.

In 1995, the web suddenly seemed to catch on in the UK; everyone was going online, and there was extensive media coverage about using the internet. Their website's traffic grew significantly in a short time, doubling every two weeks, which made it more difficult for them to run their movie database website as a volunteer hobby. So, Col and his team decided to start a company and divide the shares on a fair basis amongst the twenty volunteers spread throughout the world. None of them thought the shares would be worth anything. They incorporated IMDb, Internet Movie Database limited, with Col as the CEO in the UK.

IMDb team bought their first web servers on a credit card, which they soon maxed out. Even so, they still needed more servers. One of their team members lived in Wisconsin, United States. He went to a local internet service provider and asked if they would host a copy of IMDb in exchange for free promotion on their home page. That company took the deal, so they shipped all IMDb's software and data on a four-gigabyte hard disk to Wisconsin.

IMDb.com was launched shortly before the Oscars in 1996. A couple of weeks later, Col got a call from their first ad customer. He had never sold any advertising before and suggested an arbitrary price. The client agreed right away, and the money was more than enough to pay off their credit card before it was due. They immediately used the extra cash to triple their servers. A couple of months later, they sold their first piece of advertising to a film studio; 20th Century Fox bought an ad for the movie "Independence Day." After movie studios started buying advertising from IMDb, Cole quit his day job and became the first official employee of IMDb. Whenever IMDb's revenue went up and could afford another salary, they hired another volunteer shareholder as a full-time employee.

One day, Col got an email from a person at a small Seattle-based company called Amazon. The email said, "Hi Cole, my boss Jeff Bezos and I were discussing movie websites the other day, and IMDb came up in our conversation. Jeff and I will be in the UK in January, and we would love to meet to discuss some business ideas." Col agreed to the meeting, thinking it would be about an advertising deal.

Col and one of his colleagues met with Jeff Bezos, Amazon's CEO, in his hotel in London. Jeff told them a little bit about the history of Amazon and then said, "I assume you know why we called this meeting." Cole said, "Is it to talk about an advertising deal?" Jeff laughed and then explained how amazon.com would be going from selling eBooks to music and videos. He shared that Amazon intended to open a store selling VHS tapes and those new shiny round things called DVDs. In January 1998, Amazon was still an online bookseller, and it had never purchased or acquired a company before. Jeff was looking for a website to partner with, and the partnership could be anything from a licensing deal all the way to acquisition. Jeff told Col that IMDb could stay a separate brand, and at the same time, Amazon would use IMDb's database to build the world's best video store. Jeff had such a clear picture of how IMDb could sit within the bigger Amazon family that they found themselves agreeing in principle. After that meeting, Col and some of the other principal shareholders went out to Seattle and met the Amazon team. After lots of negotiations with lawyers in the UK, IMDb became a wholly-owned subsidiary of Amazon in April of 1998. Amazon kept Cole running IMDb and hired all of the other volunteer shareholders. Later that year, Amazon launched its video store.

A few years later, Amazon launched downloadable digital movies and then Prime Video and Amazon Studios. IMDb was added to Kindle tablets and Fire TV interface. Building upon the things that

Amazon made, IMDb has been growing within the Amazon environment ever since it was acquired. IMDb now helps power some of the Alexa entertainment queries. As of 2022, Col Needham is still the CEO of IMDb, which has added more than eight million titles to its database.

Some years after starting IMDb, Col talked to his grandmother about it and said, "It's all the result of that coloring competition I won." She looked at him and said, "I have a terrible confession; after you went to bed that night, I couldn't help but to color in all the bits that you missed and go over the things that were in the wrong color!" She couldn't resist ensuring that her grandson would win the big trip to the cinema!

Chapter 18

Go Golfing

The Story of Instagram's Founders

"You can spend all the time you want, but by the time you figure it out, you're dead."
—*Anonymous*

Instagram is a free social media platform for sharing photos and videos. Since its launch, Instagram has become a popular way to connect with friends, family, celebrities, and more. From short-form videos to live streaming, Instagram has a vast array of features. Before adding those features, however, Instagram was started as a simple photo-sharing app created by Kevin Systrom and Mike Krieger in 2010.

Kevin Systrom grew up in Holliston, a small town outside Boston, Massachusetts. In high school, Kevin fell in love with photography, art history, and computer science and wanted to combine his passion for technology and art. When Kevin started looking at colleges, he visited universities in his own state during spring, but no one was outside. He then made a trip to California just to see the schools on the West Coast. When he got to Stanford, he saw its beautiful campus with palm trees and students enjoying the nice weather doing outdoor activities. But he also noticed that everyone there loved working hard on new interesting things. He said to himself, "I want to be in a place where people want to enjoy life but work hard too." So, he decided to move to California and go to Stanford to major in computer science.

The first course Kevin signed up for at Stanford was called "Computer Science 106 X." The X stood for extreme and was supposed to be the entire year pressed into one quarter. As a freshman, he quickly realized how challenging the course was. He worked really hard but still wasn't getting a great grade and thought maybe computer science wasn't for him. Eventually, he decided to switch to a management science major. Still, he kept practicing coding on the side the entire time he was at Stanford, even though he did not take the classes.

Because of his love for art history and photography, Kevin went to Florence, Italy, to study for a semester. While there, he didn't have much to do after class because it was winter and very cold. But it was a perfect time for him to start his first entrepreneurial venture. Kevin knew that new students were looking to get a fridge and other stuff for their rooms every year. However, there was a mismatch; at the end of the year, people wanted to get rid of the stuff, while at the beginning of the year, everyone wanted to buy those stuff. So Kevin decided to make a website, like an exclusive Craigslist for Stanford's students, to fill the gap. During that winter in Italy, Kevin taught himself a new programming language, learned about databases, and built his website on his laptop. The house he was in had no Wi-Fi, so he had to go out in the cold to a library to send emails to people back at Stanford to promote his website. A thousand Stanford students signed up for it, but only a few used it. Even though his first startup idea didn't work out, Kevin got some experience making a program and marketing a consumer website.

Kevin really wanted to experience working for a startup and started looking for an internship when his website didn't work out. He found a startup named Odeo, which later became Twitter, on the New York Times website's front cover. He thought that was interesting and found its founder Evan Williams' email address on a hacker website. He sent Evan a note but didn't hear anything back. So Kevin kept sending more emails until Evan replied back, "All right, we'll talk when you're back." The following summer, Kevin ended up working at Odeo, where he met people who later helped him along the way.

Graduation was drawing closer, but Kevin wasn't sure what he wanted to do after college. His classmates were interviewing at investment banks and consulting firms and getting offer letters with six figures. Kevin wanted to work on a startup, but his parents insisted that he should find a more stable job. Most of his friends with computer science majors were going to Google, which seemed like a great place to learn and work. So, Kevin decided to go to Google after graduation. Kevin applied for the product manager job at Google that he really wanted. But Google wouldn't hire him because he didn't have a computer science degree. He had other job offers from some startups and Microsoft. However, he was willing to take even the lowest salary just to work at Google. Kevin didn't care what job it was; he just wanted to surround himself with brilliant people. He finally managed to get a job as an associate product marketing manager at Google. It was more of a marketing job than a technical role. Still, in that position, Kevin got the chance to work on Gmail, Google calendar, and spreadsheets while learning a lot about business and marketing.

After some time, Kevin moved to the corporate development group at Google, which was tasked with investing in and buying companies. After doing that for about a year, he realized many people were having a lot of fun starting companies. Then 2008 came, and the economy crashed. Kevin could still find many interesting companies and startups for acquisitions, but, every time he suggested those companies to his boss, he said, "We're not going to do many deals at this time. You should just go golfing to spend some time enjoying yourself." As a young guy in his twenties, Kevin wanted to make a difference in the world. But when his boss told him to go golfing, he realized that he should quit his corporate job and follow his passion for small companies. So finally, Kevin quit his Google job and joined a startup founded by some former Google employees called Nextstop.

He started with a marketing position there and then worked his way to programming. In the end, Kevin became a full-time engineer working on marketing problems. It was a hugely beneficial experience because he learned how to professionally program and build a website.

After gaining that valuable experience, Kevin decided to start his own company, Burbn. Burbn was a location-sharing app that people could use to check in. As part of the check-in, people could attach a photo or a video. His friends from Google introduced him to some investors, and Kevin made a prototype and showed it to one of them. He liked it and invested $50,000 in his company. Kevin was so excited that he immediately called his parents and said, "I'm going to do my own startup!" then he kept talking to more people, raising half a million dollars.

Kevin was by himself at Burbn in the beginning. After getting funds, he started looking for a co-founder and found Mike Krieger. Mike was from Brazil, and it took a month to get a visa for him. Meanwhile, Kevin was trying different ideas on Burbn. When Mike finally came to the US, they sat down, and Kevin said, "I think we have to focus on photos instead of location-sharing." Mike had just left his job in Brazil to join Burbn, and now Kevin was telling him that they needed to do something else. They worked on a photo-sharing prototype for about a week before deciding their photo app was terrible and going back to building location check-ins. However, something about photos kept drawing them back. At that time, several startups and companies were working on check-in apps. The difference with Burbn was that people could post a photo along with their check-ins. That was what people really loved about Burbn, not the check-in feature. So, Kevin and Mike once again decided to cut everything else and only focus on photos. But most people they talked to didn't think photo sharing was innovative enough to be any money in it.

After working for about seven months on Burbn, Kevin and Mike finally knew that it would not work and began focusing full-time on their new app called Instagram. They worked on Instagram for a while, but it wasn't going anywhere. Kevin felt that he needed a break to clear his mind, so he went to Mexico with his girlfriend for a vacation. One day in Mexico, they walked along the beach and talked about Kevin's new app. Kevin's girlfriend said, "I don't like posting my pictures because they aren't that great. I don't know how your friend takes these beautiful photos." Kevin said, "Well, that's because he uses software that filters photos." She said, "Oh, then you should probably add filters." Kevin thought maybe she was right. Kevin was familiar with filters from a photography class in Florence. When Kevin and his girlfriend went back to their rental place in Mexico, Kevin used their dial-up internet to research how to change the look of pixels in an image. That afternoon, he built a filter, took a photo with it, and then emailed that photo to Mike; it looked great!

When Kevin came back, he and Mike started thinking about what mattered most in photo-sharing. They noticed that other photo-sharing apps were very slow, and the photos needed some modification to improve their look. They concluded that to make their photo-sharing app successful, they needed to focus on three things: being fast, having beautiful photos, and enabling distribution everywhere, like Facebook. They made filters so that everyone could take attractive pictures. And to make their photo-sharing fast, they used a simple technique; while someone was choosing a filter and filling out the caption, the app would start uploading in the background. So, when they clicked after entering a caption, the photo would be posted right away. Lastly, they added features to allow users to easily share their photos across multiple networks all at once.

It took Kevin and Mike about eight weeks to build the first version of Instagram. Kevin thought Instagram would become popular with designers and photographers, so he emailed a hundred of them and got every one of them to sign up for the beta version. Most of them liked the app and started talking about it with their friends. Kevin and Mike finally launched Instagram in the app store at midnight on October 6, 2010. People instantly started signing up. Kevin thought, "It's 12:30 am; who's up installing apps right now?!" The first giant set of their users were all from Asia and Europe. After a year, Burbn had only 10,000 people in total. On the other hand,

Instagram had 25,000 people sign up on day one, and it just kept going.

A month after launching, Instagram had grown to one million users. Over time, Instagram rolled out features to allow users to upload short videos, follow other users' feeds, tag locations, and comment on other users' pictures and videos. For two years, Kevin, Mike, and a small team of a few engineers ran the company until Facebook acquired Instagram for $1 billion in cash and stock in April 2012. Kevin owned 40% of Instagram going into the deal. According to Forbes, Kevin mainly got Facebook stock, making him a young billionaire in a couple of years. Kevin and Mike continued running Instagram as its CEO and CTO and helped Instagram become a fast-growing app with roughly one billion monthly users. However, after some disagreements with other Facebook executives, Kevin Systrom and Mike Krieger resigned from Instagram in September 2018.

Chapter 19

Public Intellectual

The Story of LinkedIn's Founder

"Brilliant thinking is rare, but courage is in even shorter supply than genius."
—*Peter Thiel*

L inkedIn is the world's largest online professional network. People can use LinkedIn to find the right job, make professional relationships, or learn the skills they need for their careers. Now owned by Microsoft, LinkedIn was founded by Reid Hoffman in 2003.

Reid Hoffman was born in 1967 in Palo Alto, California, where his father was a law student at Stanford University. From an early age, Reid got into board and fantasy role-playing games. Around the age of nine, he became obsessed with "Dungeons and Dragons" and spent every waking hour playing it. By chance, the company that made Dungeons and Dragons was located in Berkeley, where Reid lived growing up. He spent most of his afternoons visiting that gaming company until they finally employed him to edit the scenario packs. He got his first paycheck by working on a fantasy role-playing game while also learning strategy by playing those very same games.

Reid was a terrible student until the end of seventh grade. He got an F in French because he would read science fiction books during the entire class. Around age thirteen, he realized that he would be responsible for himself after high school, and he needed to figure out what he wanted to do. He thought, "What is my plan when I get out of high school?" The only thing that he could think of at the time was that most of the people with interesting lives went to college. He decided he should go to a good college, which meant he needed to do well in high school, so he shifted entirely to studying in eighth grade.

Reid wanted to learn to be independent, so he applied for a boarding school in Vermont without his parents knowing. After he got accepted, he went to his dad and said, "I'd like to go to this boarding school." His father said, "That's fine. But wait a minute, where is that?" Reid replied, "It's in Vermont." His father then said, "Let's talk about this a little bit." Having lawyer parents, Reid had to make a case whenever he wanted something from a very early age. Reid convinced his parents to let him go to Vermont, thinking that independence would be fun. Yet, the boarding school turned out to be a challenging environment, and the first year was one of the hardest of his life. Despite the challenges, it was very instructive and taught Reid how to overcome difficulties and experience a broad range of new things; he did blacksmithing, woodworking, drove oxen, and farmed maple syrup. But after being gone for three years, he felt it was time to return to the Bay Area after graduation.

After returning home, Reid decided to go to Stanford University because there was a program called "Structured Liberal Education," which was a combination of philosophy, history, art, psychology, and sociology. Reid found that program appealing because he wanted to become a public intellectual and participate in the public discussion about who humans were and who they should be as individuals and society. Academia seemed like the right way to do it, so he planned to write books and become a philosophy professor to share his ideas with the world.

After finishing college, Reid got a scholarship from Oxford University and went there to study philosophy as a master's student.

In his first term at Oxford, he got an assignment to write an essay about human identity. His advisor's feedback was that his writing wasn't professional and had nothing to do with academic philosophy, which made him realize that being in academia wasn't the public intellectual pursuit he had hoped for. After years of thinking about an academic career, Reid realized that he needed to do something else. Oxford University allowed him to do his master's in three years, rather than the typical two. In the second year, he did minimum academic work to maintain his status as a legitimate student while spending the rest of his time thinking about what path would work for him. Reid then remembered being exposed to entrepreneurship, technology, and software at Stanford and decided he could use software instead of books and essays to communicate and change society. The problem, however, was that he had no idea how to do that. He had done some coding but had never professionally written a program. So, he decided to reconnect with his friends from Stanford and ask them what they knew.

Reid got his master's degree in philosophy from Oxford in 1993 and moved back into his dad's apartment in the Bay Area. After about three weeks, his dad said, "When are you going to go get a job?" Reid said, "Well, I'm researching." His dad said, "No, go get a job." Reid said okay and contacted one of his friends who worked at Apple. As the online revolution was about to begin in 1993, Apple started a project called "eWorld," and Reid's friend was luckily working on that project. When Reid asked him about getting a job at Apple, he said, "You don't have the typical skill set, but you are a smart person and should be able to help with our problems. If you're willing to do the contract to hire thing, we can see if it works out." After joining Apple, Reid wrote out a long list of skills he thought he would need to create a product, then started volunteering for projects that would allow him to learn and apply those skills. He ultimately worked his way into the product management team at Apple; however, that was during Apple's downturn, and the eWorld project eventually collapsed.

After Apple, Reid got a product management job at Fujitsu, which allowed him to practice all the skills he had learned. But he realized that he would have to start his own business if he was going to create the products he wanted to. So, he quit his job in 1997 and started his first startup called "SocialNet," which involved forming connections and bringing people together around a common cause. However, in 1997, it was still the early edge of the internet. At the time, SocialNet's board thought all the successful companies had to run television advertising campaigns, but Reid believed the opposite. Because of their disagreements, the board lost their confidence in him, and Reid decided to resign and start a new company. Reid was friends with PayPal's co-founder Peter Thiel and talked to him about his plan for founding a new company. Peter told him, "No, come join us. PayPal will probably be acquired within six months. Come and help us sort out our business, and then go start your own company," so Reid joined PayPal.

In the beginning, PayPal was a payment solution for transferring money on Palm Pilots. But all of a sudden, eBay sellers started using it. PayPal's team pivoted entirely from focusing on Palm Pilots to email payments, but eBay had its own payment system competing with PayPal. Reid's job was to ensure that eBay wouldn't drive PayPal off its platform. He was also responsible for working with the federal government to resolve PayPal's legal challenges. PayPal was a disruption to banking, a very established and regulated industry, and hence they had multiple regulation issues. One of them was that New York's Attorney General was suing PayPal for money laundering because they were convinced PayPal was being used for gambling. Reid had to talk to regulators and persuade them that what they were doing wasn't illegal.

In the summer of 2000, PayPal burned millions of dollars every month, so some of its co-founders, Peter Thiel, Max Lavchin, and Luke Nosek, decided to go offsite with Reid to figure out their strategy. They stayed at Reid's grandparents' place in Northern California. The first day they asked, "What should we do with PayPal?" They decided that PayPal had to be a master merchant and take fees for accepting electronic payments. On the second day, they presented their ideas on what else they could do if PayPal didn't work out. Reid talked about his idea for a social network for professionals. He said,

"Everyone's going to have a public, professional identity that will be useful to their career." His idea had some of the components of what later became LinkedIn. They put aside business and went hiking on the third day because they knew that it would be their last day off for a while. Eventually, their idea worked, and PayPal became a successful payment system. But they still had difficulty growing their profitability on eBay, and the synergies of putting these two companies together became very obvious. Ultimately in 2002, PayPal was sold to eBay for $1.5 billion.

After PayPal sold to eBay, Reid left the company and decided to take a year off and travel around the world. He started his vacation by going to Australia with one of his friends. However, after spending just two weeks in Australia, he realized that it wasn't wise to take a long vacation at that time. In 2002, most people in Silicon Valley thought that the consumer internet was over post dot-com crash. Most believed that companies like Amazon, Google, eBay, and Yahoo, which survived the dot-com crash, would be the whole consumer internet, and it was the time for investors and entrepreneurs to look at other things, like enterprise software or cleantech. Yet Reid believed that the consumer internet was just starting and there was a big opportunity to create a company during that economic downturn and that he might never have a chance like that again. Reid finished his break in two weeks instead of a year and went back to Silicon Valley, where he spent about two months thinking about different ideas and what he could do. In the end, he realized that LinkedIn was still the best idea he'd had, so he talked to some of his friends about it. They all liked it and came together to start working on it.

LinkedIn was incorporated in early 2003 and launched later that year. About 2,000 people signed up for the service each week in the first two months, which was not impressive for a social network. They worked for a year to solve LinkedIn's growth problem. After getting more acceptable user numbers, they had to deal with another problem; not having a revenue stream. They came up with job listings, so people could use LinkedIn for finding a job and recruiting and assumed that would become a big revenue source for LinkedIn.

However, it didn't turn out to be the case, and only a few people bought job listings from LinkedIn. They then started selling subscriptions and ads, which pushed LinkedIn to profitability by the end of 2005.

Reid stayed as LinkedIn's founding CEO for the first four years before becoming president of products in 2007, then executive chairman in 2009. LinkedIn went public in 2011 and was later acquired by Microsoft for $26 billion in 2016. At the time of acquisition, LinkedIn had hundreds of millions of users worldwide, and since then, it has remained the biggest social network platform for professionals.

Besides founding LinkedIn, Reid invested in and joined consumer internet companies' boards since leaving PayPal in 2002. He has invested in some successful companies like Airbnb and Facebook, contributing to his multi-billion-dollar wealth. Reid Hoffman has also served on several nonprofit boards and co-authored three books titled "The Start-Up of You," "Masters of Scale," and "The Alliance," in which he shared the entrepreneurship lessons he learned throughout his career.

Chapter 20

From Farm Boy to the Big City

The Story of Medium's Founder

"My life's mission is to hook up the 5.5 billion brains on this planet."
—*Dave Hughes*

Medium.com, co-founded by Evan "Ev" Williams and launched in 2012, is an open writing platform where bloggers can write, publish, and promote their stories to a vast audience of millions both on and off Medium. It allows its users to follow their favorite writers, and anyone can be an individual contributor.

Ev Williams grew up on a farm full of cornfields outside Clarks in Nebraska, a tiny rural area in the middle of the country. Ev felt different from his peers in many ways growing up there. All the boys played football except him in high school, making him feel he didn't belong there and yearn for the world outside. He felt isolated because there was no internet access back then, and he never traveled anywhere. Books were the only things that could take him out of his hometown, so he read all the books he could find at the library, from how to juggle to Benjamin Franklin's biography.

When Ev was fifteen, his dad got an IBM computer and some

proprietary farm applications. Ev was very excited and read the manual to teach himself how to work with the computer. Around the same time, he took the required introductory programming class in high school and learned basic programming, going way beyond his assignments and becoming very good at coding. For Ev, it was the best thing he had ever done. But he didn't know how to make the IBM at home do what the Apple computer did at school, so when everybody left the school and shut the lights off, he would remain there to continue programming.

Because of his passion for computers in high school, Ev wanted to become a computer programmer. Instead, in 1990, he went to the University of Nebraska-Lincoln, the same school his family members had attended, because he wasn't sure what else to do. Ev always knew he wanted to be independent and start his own company, so although he was enrolled in college for two years, he didn't take it seriously. He went to the first week of classes both semesters of his second year to get the student loan money and then stopped going and dropped out.

After dropping out of college, Ev started a company with his dad and brother making CDs of an encyclopedia for the Nebraska Cornhuskers football team, the most exciting thing someone could do in Nebraska. They bought a CD burner, which was expensive back then, and got a license from the University of Nebraska to make CDs with videos and pictures. However, it turned out that the overlap of Nebraska football fans and those who had CD readers wasn't large in 1993. Ev's brother had to keep many of those CDs in his garage for a long time, and they barely broke even.

While Ev was searching for something else to do, he saw a new computer magazine in a store. It was the second-ever issue of Wired magazine published in early 1993. He picked it up, thinking it must have something to do with computers. But that Wired magazine was not just about computers; it was about a new world called the internet. Ev became fascinated with an article about Dave Hughes, who was working on wiring up the internet. That Wired magazine gave Ev a glimpse of a whole other world when he was 20 years old.

Ev saw the internet as the future and thought he had to be there for it, so he recruited some of his friends and founded his first internet company in Lincoln. However, their first product was VHS tapes to teach people how to use the internet. But when Ev started his internet company in 1993, no one in his town knew anything about it. After those teaching videos didn't take off, they started looking for new ideas, but none of them really knew how to write software. So, Ev and his friends taught themselves HTML and opened a website development shop while trying to find local customers. Ev learned a lot in that company, but he lost a good deal of his father's money and finally shut the company down in 1996.

Through the magazines, Ev knew that all the internet things were happening in the San Francisco Bay Area and decided he had to be there. His girlfriend had gotten a job and moved there six months before, and when Ev had helped her move to California, he saw the possibilities. Unfortunately, Ev didn't have any money at that time, so he started looking for his first professional job. He finally got employment at a book publisher called O'Riley, based in Sebastopol, a tiny town an hour north of San Francisco.

When Ev was in Nebraska, he thought Sebastopol was very close to San Francisco. But once he got there, he realized that it was a little far away from the city and action. When his older sister came to visit shortly after he moved to California, they stayed at a hotel in downtown San Francisco with a panoramic view of the city. As they looked out over the city, Ev said it would have been amazing if he could move there. Ev was still broke from his first company, and his sister paid for their drinks with her salary as a school teacher. But she encouraged Ev to move to San Francisco. For a farm boy, moving to the big city was a scary but exhilarating thought.

Ev finally moved to San Francisco to be closer to the action. He had learned enough programming, and there was enough demand to get a job. He started doing contract development for HP and Intel, big companies that hired consulting firms to build internet applications. He made $50 an hour for his first contract, which was the most he'd ever been paid in his life. For his next contract, his fee rose to $85 per hour. He didn't know what to do with all that money.

Still, he hated his job because while Ev liked the coding, he didn't care about the projects he was working on. He once again began thinking about starting his own business. To follow his passion, Ev founded a startup to make project management software with two of his friends.

While working on their software, Ev and his friends created a note-taking feature that could be used for blogging. Back then, only a few people had personal websites, and some of them converted their sites into weblogs, an online diary with the most recent posts showing up first at the top. Ev had a personal website since 1996, mostly to work on his HTML skills and write about his personal thoughts. Still, back then, most didn't know how to publish their thoughts on the internet. So, in August 1999, Ev and his friends launched Blogger, a free platform that allowed users to create a blog from a template, as a side project. It was one of the first web applications for creating and managing weblogs. They immediately got attention from the blogging community and started getting press. A year later, they launched Blog-Spot.com, the host of Blogger. People could choose their domain name and start posting their thoughts on BlogSpot. It skyrocketed in popularity as it made blogging much simpler.

Blogger was self-funded for a year. One person on the trio team would hold a day job and pay the bills for all of them, while the other two friends worked on the startup. Then they would switch. After the first year, they raised $500,000 from O'Riley and hired more people with that money to expand their company, but they soon ran out of that money, and then the dot-com crash happened in 2000. Unfortunately, the bubble had popped entirely, so Blogger's investors were out, and there was no more money to go around by the end of 2000. Since they couldn't pay the team anymore, everyone left Blogger except Ev, who decided to keep working on it. Despite the funding issues, Blogger was still growing, so Ev called for donations from their users. He got $14,000 from the users and bought three faster servers with that money. Blogger was run mainly by Ev the first year after the layoff. He then gradually started hiring other people again. Two years later, things were going much better, and Ev sold Blogger to Google with an all-stock purchase deal around the end of 2002. Blogger was the first company that Google acquired.

After the acquisition, Ev joined Google and started working there. Blogger acquisition took place at precisely the same time as the pilot launch of Google AdSense, which was supposed to replace the ad banners and was the most important project at Google. Since everyone was focused on the AdSense project, Ev felt that Google had no plan for Blogger, and they were basically left on their own to figure out how to grow. He wasn't particularly well-versed in how to navigate inside a big company. Still, he kept working there for another two years. Eventually, Blogger grew to tens of millions of users and was secure enough that Ev felt his work was done there.

After leaving Google in 2004, Ev co-founded a podcast company named Odeo. But after a few months, it appeared that the idea wasn't really working, so Ev and his co-founders decided to pivot and started working on some small side projects. Among those projects was Twitter, a free social networking and micro-blogging service. Twitter was spun out as a new company in spring 2007, with Ev as co-founder, board member, and investor. A year later, Ev became CEO of Twitter, succeeding Jack Dorsey in October 2008.

Two years later, Ev stepped down from the Twitter CEO position because he wanted to get back to blogging and had many ideas he wanted to write about but couldn't as CEO of Twitter. He wasn't happy when he checked back in on Blogger and realized that it hadn't evolved much in the last ten years. Ev thought blogging was crucial because it would enable people to openly express their thoughts and ideas on a forum available to everyone. He had a clear vision for a publishing platform where people could read and write stories and ideas and attract as many voices from around the world as possible. But he was investing in other startups at that time and wasn't sure if he was ready to start a new company. He also thought he needed to focus on something different for a while, so he put his idea off. After six months, however, Ev realized that he was still obsessed with blogging, and there was a huge opportunity to be explored.

Ev decided to work with some of his friends from Twitter and build a platform to make it as easy as possible to put thoughts out onto the internet. They wanted to aggregate thoughtful content from individuals who had something to say, no matter who they were. They also created a feedback mechanism to help things reach the right audience. In 2012, they launched Medium.com, a better platform for most people than creating their own blog.

Medium proliferated, reaching about 13 million unique consumer users in a year. Ev believed that Medium's main goal wasn't to benefit companies by marketing, so he made the hard decision to include no ads and no partnerships with brands. Instead, they would get the money from the end-users, who were the individuals. They launched a consumer subscription, charging users a voluntary subscription fee to read unlimited locked stories on the platform. Parts of the subscription revenue are then shared with the content creators.

In 2019, Ev stepped down from his role as a Twitter board member to focus on Medium, which since its public lunch, has grown to be one of the largest open publishing platforms on the web.

Chapter 21

Movies by Snail Mail

The Story of Netflix's Founders

"Good is the enemy of great."
—Jim Collins

These days, everyone is familiar with the video streaming platform Netflix. You've likely even heard the expression "Netflix and chill." Netflix's subscription-based service allows its users to watch TV shows and movies without commercials on a device connected to the internet, including smart TVs, game consoles, smartphones, and tablets. Netflix was founded by Reed Hastings and Marc Randolph in 1997 in Scotts Valley, California.

In 1985, Reed Hastings was a high school math teacher overseas without any computer skills. After three years of teaching in Africa, he started looking for something more exciting. There was a lot of hype around artificial intelligence in the mid-80s, and Reed found out about it through math papers he read. He thought that was what he was looking for and decided to get into computer science to work on them. Reed took a programming class at night and then started looking for jobs related to computers. However, the only job he could get was serving coffee at a computer company, which was an early innovator in using the internet and became the first company in the world to get a dot-come internet address in 1986.

Despite his menial position, Reed got the chance to learn all the early internet tools while working there. Still, he knew that he needed a degree in computer science to really break into the field, so he applied to MIT and Stanford. A few months later, Reed got into the Stanford graduate school of computer science without any computer background. Having grown up on the East Coast, he knew nothing about California when he moved there. Over the next two years, he met many people at Stanford and in Silicon Valley who had successfully started companies, and Reed thought if they could do it, so could he.

Reed started his first company when he was still at Stanford. He thought that the process of going back and forth to the mouse while typing was inefficient and wanted to make it faster, so he came up with the idea of a foot mouse! He thought he had the perfect business idea, but after using the foot mouse for a few minutes, people's legs got really sore, and the mouse got really dirty. What he thought would be the transformation of human productivity turned out to be disastrous.

After graduating, Reed worked at a wide range of companies for the next couple of years, including a startup as an engineer. Reed loved writing code and often stayed all night long working. He would always let the coffee cups build up over the week, and then every weekend, the janitor would clean all of them. After about a year and a half, Reed came into work very early one morning, thinking he was the only one there. As he walked into the bathroom, he saw his company's CEO was cleaning all his coffee cups. Reed asked, "Have you been cleaning my cups all year?" The CEO said, "Yes!" Reed asked, "Why?" The CEO said, "You work so hard, and this is the only thing that I can do for you!" Reed started thinking that they had been working for almost two years with this CEO as their leader, and although they had built an elaborate product, they couldn't figure out the market fit. He realized that true leadership was about having good judgment, not just humility.

In 1991, Reed started his own company, Pure Software, which made products for troubleshooting software, and it was on a successful track in the 1990s. Every year they offered great products, and their sales doubled. Yet, the company's growth proved challenging for Reed. He was good at figuring out the product-market fit, but he knew very little about leading a company or making enterprise sales. He resigned from the CEO job twice and said to the board that they should get someone else for that position, but the board rejected his resignation and asked him to remain as the CEO both times.

In 1995, Pure Software went public, and two years later, it was acquired by a larger competitor. Reed was disappointed after his company was acquired, and felt it was a failure, so he decided to take a break and go back to Stanford to study business while reflecting on what he wanted to do next. He initially thought he would be just an angel investor and fund several startups. But, while waiting for regulators to approve the acquisition of his company, Reed and one of his colleagues at Pure Storage, Marc Randolph, started searching for new concepts.

Every morning, Reed and Mark left their houses in Santa Cruz and drove for about 45 minutes to their office in Sunnyvale while brainstorming and talking about their ideas. They worked on those ideas during the day, and then on their way back home, they would discuss what they had found out. Their new startup idea came from a minor inconvenience: Reed got a $40 late fee for a rental movie tape. He was frustrated about paying such a large late fee and thought he couldn't be the only one struggling with this, and other people most likely had the same problem. After telling Mark about his experience, the idea of selling and renting videos by mail while eliminating all late fees dawned on them.

Reed and Mark weren't confident that their idea was doable in reality. At that time, videos were recorded on large VHS cassettes, which were heavy and expensive. But while debating the feasibility of renting out videos by mail, they coincidently read about a brand-new DVD technology. DVDs were much lighter than videotapes, so they thought they could change everything. Before driving to work one day, Reed and Mark went to a record store in Santa Cruz and bought a music CD because the DVD was not available yet. They put the CD into a small envelope, addressed it to Reed's house, and dropped it in the mail. The next day, Reed received the envelope with the intact CD. They realized right away that their crazy idea could actually work.

After spending the next few days studying different aspects, Reed and Mark finally decided to give it a try. Reed invested about $2 million of his money to start the company. They then hired some people, got a small office, and began working. In April 1997, they launched the Netflix website to rent and sell DVDs by mail. It was the world's first online DVD rental store, with a few hundred titles available, almost the entire catalog of DVDs at the time. The sale of DVDs was so good that 99% of their revenue came from selling DVDs by the end of their first summer. They were not happy with that, though, because they knew it was a commodity business, which meant they would be out of business soon if large companies decided to sell DVDs cheaper.

Selling and renting videos had very different logistics. Doing both of them simultaneously was extremely difficult for the Netflix team, so they decided to pick one and focus on it. Reed and Mark looked at the future and thought every retailer, including Amazon and Walmart, would soon be selling DVDs. They thought, "If that happens, our margins will be driven down to zero, and we would be out of business." On the other hand, the rental had good potential; it was highly differentiated and had decent margins. The problem, however, was that it wasn't as popular with the customers. Even though selling was paying the bills, they looked at the bigger picture and walked away from sales, betting everything on doing rental work.

Netflix introduced the monthly subscription concept in 1999 and then dropped the single-rental model in early 2000. They were trying to build a reputation with flat-rate, unlimited rentals without due dates and late fees. They had started right in the middle of the first internet bubble, so they were able to quickly raise some money. But then the dot-com bubble crashed before they were profitable, so they had to do a big layoff, despite trying every promotion and discount they could think of to make their business model profitable.

In 2000, two and a half year old Netflix was still a small company with less than a hundred employees. They were on track to make $10 million in revenue that year. Still, they were going to lose a cumulative $50 million. So they started seeking alternatives and decided to reach out to Blockbuster, one of their biggest competitors. Blockbuster was the number one provider of rental videos in 2000, offering its services primarily at its video rental shops and earning $6 billion in revenue with about 60,000 employees and 9000 stores. Mark and Reed tried to contact Blockbuster and get a meeting. Finally, after many attempts, Blockbuster agreed to see them, so Reed and Mark went to its head-quarter in Dallas, Texas, and pitched their idea for collaboration to its executives. They proposed to run the online business for Blockbuster, so Blockbuster could keep focusing on their stores. Some Blockbuster executives were interested in that idea and asked how much they wanted. Reed offered a price of $50 million, which Blockbuster executives thought was too much, so Reed and Mark went back home to California without any deal.

By 2004, Blockbuster realized that the DVD-by-mail trend that Netflix had started was really catching on, so they started competing very hard. Blockbuster had an advantage in having lower prices than Netflix because of its stores, but when Netflix and Blockbuster got into a multiyear, brutal battle for market share, it was unclear who would win. During that time, Netflix's stock dived, going down from $39 to $9. However, the Netflix team stayed focused and kept making their service better. Eventually, Netflix picked up momentum because it offered more selection and better integration with the post office, and by 2009, Blockbuster had given up and withdrawn from the rental DVD market. A year later, Blockbuster went bankrupt and disappeared completely.

While competing with Blockbuster, Netflix started a new way of delivering movies to its customers: streaming. The streaming website YouTube, launched in 2005, paved the way. When Reed used YouTube for the first time, he was shocked; watching a video was as easy as just a click. It was like television, except people could instantly decide what to watch. Although the early version of YouTube was low quality, it still revealed that the internet was ready for streaming. So, in 2007, Netflix launched a service in the US to stream movies and television shows to computers. It barely worked! Users had to install special windows software and drivers to watch Netflix, but they made the service a little better year by year, and eventually, Netflix became browser-based.

By 2010, Netflix streaming was gaining some real momentum and had expanded internationally to Canada. It was their first time providing service without DVDs, which worked well, and right away, people started using the streaming service. Netflix then successfully expanded into thirty countries in Latin America in 2011. At that point, they decided to split the company and make their DVD business into a new brand. DVDs was still eighty percent of their revenue and a hundred percent of their profit, but they were excited about the future and wanted Netflix to become solely streaming. Unfortunately, their customers were not ready for that much change yet. Netflix increased its prices from $10 to $16 to cover its costs, which was considered a big price increase in 2011, shortly after an economic recession. That poor decision almost killed Netflix's business, but Netflix managed to get through that crisis and started expanding in Europe.

Netflix's streaming popularity kept growing over the years, and more people cut the cord and turned to streaming services for their film and television content. When the coronavirus global pandemic of 2020 forced lockdowns worldwide, even more people turned to Netflix for streaming movies and TV shows at home, while most other forms of entertainment were closed. As a result, Netflix recorded a jump in new users, leading to a record year of new customers. Today, Netflix is a global entertainment company in more than 150 countries and produces its own critically acclaimed TV shows, like House of Cards and Squid Game, movies, and original comedy specials. However, the high demand for streaming services has created a streaming war, where Netflix is competing with Disney+,

HBO Max, Apple TV Plus, and Amazon Prime Videos. Despite the competition, Netflix remains the world's largest subscription streaming service, with more than 200 million paid subscribers world-wide as of 2022.

Reed Hastings revolutionized how the world is entertained by attacking TV as a whole while having fun in the process. During the 2010s, Netflix was the top-performing stock in the S&P 500 stock market index, with a total return of more than 3,000%. Reed report-edly owns about 1% of Netflix, putting him on the billionaires list. He served as the chairman and CEO of Netflix from 1999 to 2020 when it was announced that Ted Sarandos would serve as co-CEO with him. As Reed led Netflix's expansion, he also created innovative manage-ment practices and culture for the company. In September 2020, he co-authored a book on Netflix's culture and management system named "No Rules Rules: Netflix and the Culture of Reinvention." Reed is also a noted philanthropist and has devoted his time to educa-tional issues.

Chapter 22

X

The Story of PayPal's Founders

"Genius is one percent inspiration and ninety-nine percent perspiration."
—*Thomas Edison*

P ayPal is a digital system for sending and receiving money, making an online payment, or setting up a merchant account. One of the original web payments companies, PayPal was created in 2000 by the merger of two startups, Confinity, founded by Luke Nosek, Max Levchin, and Peter Thiel, and X.com, founded by Elon Musk.

Elon Musk was born in Pretoria, South Africa, in 1971. He was a quiet bookworm as a kid who read everything he could get his hands on, from when he woke up until when he went to sleep. He ran out of books at one point, so he started reading an encyclopedia. When Elon was thirteen, he had an existential crisis, so he read various books trying to figure out the meaning of life. Some of the books by Nietzsche and Schopenhauer he found in the house sounded pretty negative to a teenager like Elon. Then he read "The Hitchhiker's Guide to the Galaxy" and found it quite uplifting, sparking his interest in space.

When Elon was about nine years old, he went into a store and saw a computer for the first time. He thought that was the most incredible thing he'd ever seen. After getting his own computer, Elon realized that he could make his own games, so he bought some books to teach himself programming. Soon, he began selling the games he made just so he could buy more games and better computers. Elon and his younger brother Kimball were video game experts in their teenage years and knew all the popular games. So they decided to open a video game arcade near their high school. They got a lease on a building and had the arcade provider deliver the equipment. The only thing they needed to do was get the city to approve what they were doing. But an adult had to apply for a city permit, and they hadn't told their parents what they were up to. When their parents found out, they put a stop to it.

As Elon read more about the technology, he noticed that most innovations were happening in the United States. So one of his goals growing up was to go to America. He tried to convince his mother and father, who were divorced, that one of them should move to the United States. His father was a well-established engineer in South Africa and didn't want to move. His mother was born in Canada to an American father but hadn't gotten her American citizenship. However, since she was born in Canada, Elon could get Canadian passports for his mother, brother, and himself.

Three weeks after getting his Canadian passport, 17-year-old Elon went to Canada by himself. His father said he would not pay for college unless it was in South Africa, so he had to find some way to pay for it. He started working at odd jobs across the country before settling at Queens University in Kingston. He was there for a couple of years until he got a scholarship from the University of Pennsylvania to study business and physics. Elon then transferred to the University of Pennsylvania and finally moved to the U.S.

At college, Elon started asking himself what would most influence the future of humanity. He decided upon sustainable energy, electric cars, and space exploration, specifically making life multi-planetary, and discussed these topics with his friends, housemates, and even on dates. The first question Elon asked his girlfriend during college was, "Do you ever think about electric cars?"

Elon had been thinking about electric cars for a couple of years and wanted to do something related to them. One of his professors at the University of Pennsylvania was the chairman of a Silicon Valley company working on advanced capacitors for electric cars. Elon saw an excellent opportunity to go to Silicon Valley and work on electric vehicles with him. He got the summer job in 1994 and started doing research on electrolytic ultracapacitors. But it turned out that only a few tons of a key chemical required for them existed in the world. Their product was too expensive and not very scalable.

After arriving in Silicon Valley, one thing that got Elon's attention was the internet. He noticed how quickly it was growing and encouraged his brother Kimball, who was studying business at Queen's University in Canada, to come to Silicon Valley and do an internship related to the internet. Kimball listened to Elon and joined him in Silicon Valley, where they both got jobs at a video game company called Rocket Science. Elon held two jobs: working on ultra-capacitors for electric cars during the day, and working on video games at night.

Another thing that got Elon's attention was Stanford University. He thought of Stanford as the epicenter of Silicon Valley, and that's where he wanted to go to. He applied to Stanford University graduate school to study applied physics and material science and got admitted in the Fall of 1995. In the summer of that year, Elon returned to Silicon Valley to get a summer job. He was still thinking about those three things that would impact the world most, but he couldn't figure out how to make enough money on the internet to pursue his passions in electric cars and space exploration. His first plan was to work as a teaching assistant while completing his graduate degree and researching electric vehicle technologies. But then he thought if he did a PhD at Stanford, he would waste several years watching the internet go through an incredibly rapid growth phase.

Elon knew the internet would change the world in a major way and decided he wanted to be part of it. He first tried to get a job at Netscape and sent his resume. But he didn't get any reply because he lacked a computer science degree. He even tried hanging out in the Netscape lobby, trying to see if he could speak to someone, but he was too shy and scared to approach anyone, and left embarrassed. There were only a few internet companies in 1995, and Elon couldn't get a job at any of them. He thought, "I guess I'll have to start my own company because I can't get a job anywhere." Once again, his brother Kimball joined him. They were finishing school at the same time because Elon was doing a double major.

In the summer of 1995, the Musk brothers started their own company, called Zip2, with the initial idea of creating software that could help bring media companies online. Elon wrote software that summer, but at the start of the quarter for Stanford, he had to make a decision. He thought, "If I start a company and it doesn't work, then I can always go back to grad school." So he decided to defer. Elon talked to the department chair and said, "I'm working on my internet company. It probably won't succeed, so I want to make sure that I can still come back when it fails. I'll probably be back in six months." The department chair let Elon go on deferment and said, "I'm probably never going to hear from you again!"

At first, Elon and Kimball had low ambitions and just wanted to make enough money to pay the bills. It was cheaper to rent an office than an apartment, so they just rented a small office, slept on the couch there, and showered at the gym. They worked all the time, seven days a week, and usually ate a Jack-in-the-Box at 3:00 in the morning because it was difficult to get food in Palo Alto after 10:00 p.m. To save some money, they had just one computer, which served as the webserver during the day, and then Elon would program on it at night.

The internet was just a couple of years old when Elon started, and most people still used the Yellow Pages to find local businesses. Elon's idea was to bring newspapers into the digital age, so he took a CD of the Yellow Pages, some mapping software, and his programming skill, which he used to write code and put it all together to create the first online city listings. However, nobody was making any money on the internet in 1995, so when Elon tried to get funding for his company in November of 1995, most did not know what the internet was and had not used it. Once a senior executive threw a Yellow Pages book at him and said, "Do you really think the internet is ever going to replace this?" Everyone thought that the internet was something only universities and the government used. After Netscape went public later that year, even though venture capitalists still didn't understand and hadn't used the internet, they knew that somebody had made money on it, so it was on their radar. This sparked greater interest in what Elon and Kimball were doing when they again talked to the venture capitalists in early 1996. They closed a funding round in about one week and got three million dollars.

During the 90s, most businesses didn't have a software team and looked for other companies to develop programs for them. One of Zip2's first customers was the New York Times company Knight-Ridder. It wasn't long before other media companies across the country signed up too. In 1999, four years after Elon and his brother started, they sold the company for over 300 million dollars. One of the first things the 28-year-old millionaire did was get a sports car.

However, Elon still thought they hadn't reached the potential they could with the internet. They had created sophisticated software comparable to what Yahoo and other companies had at the time, but it wasn't getting used properly. So Elon still wanted to do something that would profoundly affect and significantly contribute to the internet. It seemed to him that the financial sector had not seen a lot of innovation on the internet, and he set his sights on it, investing most of the money he made from selling Zip2 into his next company X.com.

Elon's idea with X.com was to create an integrated set of financial services, so people could handle all their financial business from one place. They could transfer money simply by entering unique identifiers like an email address or phone number as a feature. But when he demonstrated the product, people didn't seem excited about the consolidated financial services. They were more interested in sending money by email because transactions were very slow at the time.

People back then had to mail checks to each other, so it could take weeks to complete a single transaction. So, Elon decided to focus all his energy on making online payments available.

X.com went from a financial services provider to one that offered email payments. But Elon's new company collided with a rival digital payment company called Confinity. Confinity was started by Max Levchin and Peter Thiel in 1998 as software for Palm Pilots. They then developed an application to transfer money from one Palm Pilot to another using the infrared port and a website parallel to that, which required people to synchronize their Palm Pilot to transfer via the website. It appeared people were less interested in using the Palm Pilot, but they were intrigued by the website. So, they developed a money-transfer service called PayPal to allow users to send money using email and the web.

While X.com and Confinity competed against each other, their real enemy was eBay. At some point, Elon and Confinity's founders realized that their companies had to converge to compete effectively against eBay's built-in system. In March 2000, X.com merged with Confinity under the moniker X.com. Elon was its biggest shareholder and was appointed as its CEO, a role he maintained for most of 2000. He had gotten married earlier that year and had not taken vacation or honeymoon, so he went on a combined investment-raising and honeymoon trip to Korea. But while Elon was away for two weeks, the management team decided that he wasn't the right man to run the company. Peter Thiel replaced him as the CEO.

In 2001, X.com changed its name to PayPal after its main product. PayPal faced many challenges. Various regulatory agencies tried to shut them down while they battled with Visa, MasterCard, and eBay. At the same time, the company's growth was explosive, with an exponentiating cost curve and no revenue, bringing PayPal near the point of collapse between 2000 and 2001. But PayPal had a talented group of people trying hard to keep the company solvent despite its setbacks. A year later, those efforts paid off when eBay bought PayPal for $1.5 billion in July 2002. As the largest shareholder, Elon walked away with 180 million dollars when he was 30 years old.

After selling PayPal to eBay, several PayPal co-founders and early employees started other successful internet companies. Despite the economic downturn, they all left PayPal and were free to pursue new opportunities using the capital they had gotten from PayPal. The group, known as PayPal Mafia in the media, co-founded companies such as LinkedIn, YouTube, Yelp, and the "buy now, pay later" company Affirm. But one member of the mafia wanted to go beyond the internet and digital world. In 2003, Elon was still thinking about the three things he'd thought would affect the world most when he was a student. For his next ventures, Elon was ready to go after sustainable energy, electric cars, and space exploration.

Elon wondered when humans would go to Mars. When he checked NASA's website, he realized there was no plan to go to Mars or even take the next step in space exploration. Elon thought more should be done to achieve these goals, and he got the outrageous idea that private enterprises could reenergize space travel. In June 2002, he founded Space Exploration Technologies Corporation known as SpaceX. In the early years, Elon was the only investor in the company, contributing almost a hundred million dollars which was the majority of his net worth at the time. He expected to lose all the money that he invested, but despite its setbacks in the early years, SpaceX became the first private company to send rockets, spacecraft, satellites, and even humans into orbit. As of early 2022, SpaceX is valued at about $100 billion.

In addition to exploring space, Elon wanted to make electric cars and help humanity get off fossil fuels. So he went to his cousins and told them if they started a solar power company, he would fund them. Elon's cousins took his suggestion and founded SolarCity, which produced solar energy generation systems. SolarCity soon grew into the largest solar service provider in the U.S. But renewable energy was just one part of Elon's goal. In April 2004, Elon helped launch Tesla with 6.5 million dollars of his own money. Tesla was the first auto industry startup in decades and the only one born in Silicon Valley. Elon started serving as Tesla's CEO in 2008 and since then has led the company through its difficult times. Over the years, Tesla has expedited the global move to sustainable transport and energy by creating affordable mass-market electric vehicles. Tesla shares hugely soared in 2020, making it the best performing U.S. stock and by far the most valuable automaker in the world. Tesla's market capitalization reached $1 trillion in October 2021, becoming the sixth company to reach the milestone in U.S. history.

Besides SpaceX, SolarCity, and Tesla, Elon founded several other companies after selling PayPal to eBay, including Neuralink, OpenAI, and The Boring Company. In 2015, PayPal was spun off from eBay to become an independent, publicly-traded company. As of 2022, PayPal is still one the largest fintech companies worldwide, dominating the digital payment market. Elon repurchased the domain name X.com from PayPal in 2017 because "it has great sentimental value." Through his various ventures, Elon Musk has surpassed Amazon's founder Jeff Bezos to become the richest man on the earth, with an estimated net worth of more than $250 billion.

Chapter 23

Bug Collector

The Story of Pinterest's Founders

"We don't see things as they are, we see them as we are."
—Anaïs Nin

Pinterest is a social network website where users can create virtual pinboards where they collect and share images of just about anything: weddings, home decorations, hairstyles, and so on. They can also visually discover new interests by browsing the collections of other Pinterest users. The website was founded by Ben Silbermann, Paul Sciarra, and Evan Sharp in the San Francisco Bay Area in 2009.

Ben Silbermann grew up in Iowa, outside of Des Moines. Both of his parents were doctors, so as a child, Ben thought that he would be a doctor too; he didn't really feel like he had a choice. But Ben had diverse interests from childhood and realized that he loved many other things, like nature, fiction, and movies. He also loved collecting things, especially bugs. Still, when he grew up, as expected, he went to Yale as a pre-med without any specific plan other than being a doctor.

College was the first time Ben had his own laptop with high-speed internet, which was a transformative experience for him. He fell in love with the internet because he could access all kinds of information, and after becoming more familiar with it, he started making small online tools. One of the first things he made in college was a tool for letting people try on glasses online. His parents were ophthalmologists and had an optical shop attached to their house, and Ben had watched all the people go in and try on glasses. They would try to look in the mirror, but they couldn't see, and so they would ask how these glasses looked. Ben thought maybe he could build software to help people try new glasses styles at home. While Ben's online tool didn't work out in the end, he still realized how interested he was in technology, and at one point, he finally decided that medicine wasn't really for him. When he told his parents that he didn't want to be a doctor, they said, "Okay, but figure out something to do to make money." He started taking other classes in college and ended up as a political science major.

After finishing college, Ben took a job at a consulting firm, mainly because they offered it to him and he had nothing else on his plate. He went to Washington DC and started working in the IT group at a consulting company, but he still couldn't forget his passion for technology. He always read tech news blogs and really wanted to be part of what was going on with the internet. While working in DC, he started building different things on the internet as a hobby with his friends, including a tool to help his friend's band promote themselves all over the country. But none of them were intended to be serious businesses.

Ben didn't feel that he could start his own company, but he thought working at a tech company that he respected would be a good step. He really liked Google, but the only job he could get there was online sales and operations customer support, where he would take feedback from users and feed it back into the advertisement products. Still, Ben moved out to California and worked at Google for about a year and a half, all the while still trying his own small projects on the side. Ben kept going back to the idea of building a product, but it always stalled, and he always had excuses for why. Every night he said to his girlfriend, "Wouldn't it be cool if I build this? Here's what it's going to look like," and then he would show her a simple prototype.

One night his girlfriend said, "You know Ben, maybe you should either do it or stop talking about it." It turned out to be a good piece of advice. Ben left his job at Google in May 2008 and focused on starting his own company.

Because of his background, Ben was interested in medicine and wanted to build a tool to help people gather their medical records across their families. So, he connected with some of his friends, who were mostly PhD students close to graduation, to help him create that medical family tree. Ben's friends initially had some extra time to work on things, but in a few months, they got their degrees and were going to become professors or continue their research elsewhere. So, the team fell apart, and Ben was on his own.

Ben just wandered around for some time, not doing much. But he was amazed when the iPhone came out and thought it would change everything, so he connected with one of his college friends, Paul Sciarra, to design iPhone apps together. Their idea was to make a shopping catalog by putting the mail catalogs on the phone and digitalizing them. Ben and Paul made a prototype with their savings, but they realized they needed to raise some money to continue. However, 2008 was a tough time to raise funds as it was right after the economy collapsed. That was the first time Ben had tried raising money, and it was especially hard because they were two non-technical co-founders. They went through investors from West Coast to East Coast and called everyone they could think of, even cold-calling people out of alumni directories, whether they went to the same school or not. But no one would give them any money.

Desperately looking for some funds, Ben found all the college competitions for business plans with loosely written rules about attending that particular school. They entered one of those competitions and came in second place. The prize for second place was meeting with a venture capitalist who was an alumnus of that school. Ben and his co-founder met that venture capitalist, and he gave them their first couple hundred thousand dollars. Ben couldn't believe it because it felt like all the money in the world to him. With those funds, Ben and his co-founder Paul started their company, Tote, and hired some engineers to work on their product. But developing iPhone apps and getting them approved was very slow at the time. Then, when they finally launched their app Tote, no one really used it.

During a fundraising round on the East Coast, Ben met Evan Sharp, a graduate student at Columbia University who studied architecture. Ben and Paul teamed up with Evan to work on a new idea and began thinking about what they wanted to see out there in the world. They came up with the idea of a tool to let people collect things online. Both Evan and Ben loved collecting when they were kids, so they thought having an online tool would be really fun and useful, and provide a window into how other people saw the world. They started to build an online pinboard, which eventually was named Pinterest. It was straightforward and web-based, but something that they personally would use.

Ben and his co-founders raised a little money from angel investors to start their new company. But they knew that most likely they would be without money for a while, so they decided to spend as little as possible. They got a two-bedroom apartment. Paul lived in one of the bedrooms, and they rented out the other one to a guy named Dave who had founded another startup. The two startups worked out of the living room together pretty much all day. Dave was a late-night guy and was always up until 4:00 am. When the Pinterest team had meetings with their investors or users, they would see Dave going to take a shower in his towel while waving at everyone.

Pinterest had a small team of five people who used their own personal computers. They didn't have a network of engineers in Silicon Valley, so they did all kinds of things for hiring, like posting ads on Craigslist or throwing a barbecue on their small patio every Friday to show that they were cool people. Those tricks worked, and they recruited many people on their patio. They started building Pinterest in November 2009 and launched it in March 2010. After its release, the first thing they did was email all their friends and ask them to use it. But none of them really understood what Pinterest was. Some of them thought it was interesting, but only a small group really enjoyed using it. So Ben decided to sit in a coffee shop and ask people to try his app, then watch what they were doing to see where they could improve. He also put his own cell phone number on all the customer support emails and took customer calls all the time.

Still, Pinterest was not a runaway success. It grew very slowly, and after four months, they had only about 3000 accounts, which was not very impressive for a consumer app. They noticed that many of their early users were interested in lifestyle use cases like decorating and design. So, Ben started looking into who these people were, what they read, and where they gathered. He eventually found a conference in Utah where it seemed members of his target group might be present, so he went there to meet bloggers and do a marketing campaign called "pin it forward." For a month, they invited hundreds of bloggers every day and gave them invites for their readers. Many people read those blogs, and Pinterest started growing rapidly after that. Ben and his colleagues kept the quality of the content very high and spent a ton of time making sure that all their early users had excellent experiences. They set strict rules for what was allowed on Pinterest; for example, people couldn't upload personal photos.

By 2011, Pinterest had become one of the largest social networks, and as of 2022, Pinterest has roughly 500 million users worldwide. A little over nine years after Pinterest started, the company held its IPO in April 2019, which valued the company around $12 billion, making Ben Silbermann a billionaire.

Chapter 24

Q&A Genius

The Story of Quora's Founders

"The trouble with life isn't that there is no answer, it's that there are so many answers."
—Ruth Benedict

Quora is a website that allows people to ask questions and get answers. People can follow topics, questions, and people on Quora, upvote or downvote an answer, or comment on one if they want to. Even though Quora is similar to Wikipedia or Yahoo Answers, real names are mandatory, and users need to log in or create an account there to answer questions. Quora was founded by Adam D'Angelo and Charlie Cheever in 2009.

Adam D'Angelo was known to be intelligent and a good student from early on. In 2001, he placed eighth at the USA Computing Olympiad as a high school student and was awarded a silver medal in the International Olympiad in Informatics in 2002. Adam attended the Phillips Exeter Academy in 2000, where he met Mark Zuckerberg, who later founded Facebook. During his time at the Phillip Exeter Academy, Adam and Mark instantly clicked and became friends.

Together, they developed a music suggestion software known as Synapse Media Player, which suggested music according to people's tastes. It eventually became a huge success and was acquired by Microsoft.

After high school, Adam moved to California to study computer science at the California Institute of Technology. In college, he made some internet products whenever he had spare time because he intrinsically enjoyed the work involved in making them. One of the things that he created was a website called BuddyZoo which allowed users to upload their AOL Instant Messenger buddy list and compare them with other users. When Mark Zuckerberg moved to Palo Alto for a summer after starting Facebook at Harvard to take a break from school and just focus on building Facebook, he asked Adam to join him. So Adam put his studies on hold for a while to spend a semester helping Mark during those early days of Facebook. After completing college in 2006, Adam again decided to join Mark Zuckerberg's team at Facebook as a VP of Engineering.

Besides software and computers, Adam had always been interested in social science and economics, and found Facebook a fascinating application of both computer and social sciences. He thought a lot about what motivated people to participate in these social networks and realized that people desired to signal things about themselves and provide information that could be useful to others. Facebook was a great chance to test and apply the signaling theory he had learned during college.

After a few years, Adam felt that Facebook had reached the point where it was in a really good position, and the company didn't really need him anymore. He thought he could make a bigger impact in the world by starting something new rather than just optimizing Facebook. With that in mind, Adam quit his job as the CTO of Facebook, leaving the hottest company in Silicon Valley in 2008 to start a new venture. After leaving Facebook, Adam looked around to decide what he wanted to do next. He had always been interested in knowledge sharing and questions and answers. He thought there was a tremendous amount of knowledge stored in people's heads that wasn't available on the internet. There were a lot of good ways to find information that was already on the internet, but Adam was interested in making more information available in the first place. So, he saw an opportunity to build a platform to get all this knowledge out into the world.

One thing that Adam had learned from Facebook was that execution was far more important than an idea. There had been other attempts to make knowledge-sharing websites, but it turned out to be pretty challenging to run one of these systems at scale. Yahoo Answers was one of the earliest Q&A platforms on the internet. But no experts participated there, and it had been filled with inaccurate information. Adam wanted to set up an environment where experts wished to participate.

In 2009, Adam founded Quora with Charlie Cheever, another early Facebook employee. Like Adam, Charlie Cheever has gotten into computers as a child. Charlie was at Facebook for about four years, when he too reached the point where he felt ready to start his own company. After resigning from Facebook, Adam and Charlie began working together on their new project. They used their own money initially, but raising money wasn't hard for Adam and Charlie; many investors in Silicon Valley knew them from Facebook and were willing to invest. Soon, they hired some of their other friends who were top designers and engineers at Facebook. Together, they began building Quora's online platform.

A few months after the site was ready, they decided to release the private beta for testing amongst friends through invitations. In no time, the site was creating a buzz in Silicon Valley. Friends had begun inviting others, resulting in the rapid growth of Quora's user base. One of the groups that emerged early on Quora was the startup community, who were all interested in knowledge about startups. Even Mark Zuckerberg joined that group and used Quora to ask, "What startups would be good acquisitions for Facebook?" Soon after, Facebook acquired one of the companies suggested to Mark on Quora.

From the beginning, Adam invested heavily in getting the correct answers to people and getting the questions to the right people who could write excellent answers. One of the ways they differentiated early on was that they required people to use their real names.

There was a huge spike in Quora's usage at the beginning of 2011 when it was covered by some press and endorsed by some famous people who made Quora a trending topic on Twitter. Quora had an estimated 500,000 registered users, while it had only eighteen employees. By the middle of 2011, Quora decided to redesign its website and released official Android and iPhone apps. Quora also introduced new features like threaded comments and comment voting to its Q&A pages in the same year.

In 2012, Charlie Cheever stepped down from a day-to-day role at the company while retaining an advisory role. Adam invested $20 million of his own money in the Series B round of the company's funding and acquired sufficient control over the company to have things his way. Quora introduced more new features in 2013, and at that point, it had become home to more than 16 million answers on 400,000 topics while its unique monthly visitors were proliferating. Quora has maintained its fast growth since then and reached hundreds of million monthly visitors and a valuation of $2 billion in 2019. As of 2022, Adam is still the CEO of Quora.

Since its inception, Quora has tried to maintain the reliability and accuracy of the answers provided on its platform. At the same time, its competitor Yahoo Answers became a significant source of misinformation. Yahoo Answers, one of the longest-running web Q&A platforms in the history of the internet, finally shut down in May 2021.

Chapter 25

Mmm!

The Story of Reddit's Founders

"Family's first, and that's what matters most."
—*Serena Williams*

I f you spend a lot of time online, chances are you've heard of Reddit, especially after it was thrust into the spotlight in 2021 due to its role in the GameStop trading frenzy. Reddit, famously known as the front page of the internet, is a massive collection of forums where people can share news and content or comment on other people's posts. Reddit is broken up into more than a million communities known as "subreddits," each covering a different topic. Now one of the most popular websites globally, Reddit was founded by then college students Steve Huffman and Alexis Ohanian in 2005 in Charlottesville, Virginia.

When Alexis was a teenager, he got his first job in a CompUSA store that sold everything related to computers. When one of his friends asked Alexis if he wanted a job demoing software at a CompUSA, he said sure, although he didn't know what that entailed. He took the job anyway because it paid $10 an hour. When he showed up on his first day, they put him in a little booth where he had to do the same pitch every half an hour for whatever software or hardware they had at the time. For a chubby teenager, getting up in front of an audience every half an hour and being ignored by everyone was a horrible public speaking experience. Still, he did his job and gained more self-confidence through the process.

Alexis went to the University of Virginia for college, where he met Steve Huffman in their freshman year. They lived across the hall from each other in the dorm the first year. Steve had heard that someone named Alexis lived there and thought Alexis was a girl, assuming they were in a coed dorm, but later found out that Alexis was a guy. They bonded over video games and soon became close friends.

Steve and Alexis became roommates when they were seniors at the University of Virginia. Steve was studying computer science while Alexis intended to be an immigration lawyer and was in the middle of preparing for an LSAT test. But he didn't really like the exam prep and realized that if he didn't really want to take the LSAT, he probably shouldn't be a lawyer. He would rather live like a college student working on fun projects, so he decided to become an entrepreneur. Alexis knew Steve was an engineer, and they had been bouncing ideas around for a while, so he knew they could build something together.

Steve and Alexis eventually decided to start a company, and one of their first ideas was for ordering food by cell phone. A local gas station had touch screens inside, so when someone wanted to order a sub, they would just touch a screen and place their order without talking to anyone. Steve loved that process. He used to sit there while pumping gas and think, "This is a total waste of time. I'm just standing here while the sub guy is inside and could have been making my sub right now if I could have placed an order on my phone." When Steve told Alexis his idea, he said, "We should totally build this." To make Steve's idea better, Alexis suggested giving it a catchy name, like "My Mobile Menu," abbreviated as "MMM." However, there were still no smartphones in 2005. Alexis and Steve thought to use SMS text messages to order food, so people didn't need to wait in lines, and they thought MMM could change the way people ordered food forever. So they spent their senior year hustling MMM up and down

Charlottesville and pitched it to all small restaurants. Most of those restaurants said, "That sounds good. Let us know when you got a prototype," which prompted them to start working on a prototype.

Around the same time, Steve heard that Paul Graham, one of his idols, would be giving a talk at Harvard University during spring break of their senior year. Paul Graham was a computer scientist and an entrepreneur who had authored several computer programming books. Steve told Alexis it would be cool to go to that speech. Alexis had never heard of Paul Graham but said, "Let's do it!" So instead of going to a beach during their spring break like other students at their university, Steve and Alexis went to Boston to hear Paul Graham's talk called "How to start a startup." Steve and Alexis were two undergrads planning to start a startup, and the timing couldn't have been better for them. Steve had one of Paul's books about computer programming at Paul's speech and wanted him to sign it. Alexis helped Steve get Paul's attention and started chatting him up, so Steve could get his book signed. Alexis said, "Dr. Graham, it would totally be worth the cost of buying you a drink to get your opinion on our startup. We've come all the way from Virginia." Paul was surprised and said, "You came all the way from Virginia?!" He then said, "Alright, why not? Let's meet at the cafeteria this evening."

They sat down in the cafeteria, and Paul said, "OK, let me hear your pitch." Alexis pitched him their idea for ordering food using a cell phone. Paul interrupted before he got too far into it and said their idea was fantastic, which thrilled Steve and Alexis because Paul was one of Steve's icons. They went back to Virginia feeling more confident about starting their company. A couple of days later, Steve emailed Paul to thank him for meeting with them. Paul responded, "I just started an investment company called Y Combinator. You guys should apply with your idea." Now one of the largest startup accelerators and seed-stage investment firms, Y Combinator was just a little experiment at the time. It gave early-stage startups a little bit of money to just get started and see if they could build something over a couple months. If they created something interesting, Y Combinator would introduce them to venture capitalists and other investors and try to get them off the ground.

Encouraged by Paul, Steve and Alexis went to Boston and pitched their idea to the Y Combinator team, who thought it was a pretty good one. That night, Steve and Alexis were prematurely celebrating when they got a phone call from Paul Graham; he said, "Listen, I'm very sorry, but we're going to have to reject you." They were shocked because Paul already knew their idea and had told them to apply. Alexis and Steve were very disappointed and got really drunk that night.

The next morning, they were hungover and on a train all the way back to Charlottesville when Alexis' cell phone rang; it was Paul again. Jessica Livingston, Paul's wife and one of Y Combinator co-founders, had convinced Paul to give them a chance. Paul said, "We don't like your idea, but we like you guys. If you're willing to come back, get off this train and come up with something new. We'll fund your new idea!" Steve and Alexis had spent a year in Charlottesville with restaurants to see if their idea could work, but now they had to start from scratch again. They went back up to Boston and spoke with Paul for an hour. Paul told them, "Do something on the web, not mobile phones," and then asked what their problems were every morning. They said many things, including how to find out what was going on in the world, and started developing their new idea, which later became Reddit.

In 2005, a broad array of sources created content on the internet, but there was no comprehensive aggregation. The idea behind Reddit was to be a custom selection of the most interesting of them. Steve and Alexis wanted to build a website to which anybody could submit a story, and everybody else would vote on it. Then the stories that got the highest number of votes would rise to the top. That way, people could read the selection of the most popular things every day. Paul Graham liked their new idea and told them they should make Reddit "the front page of the internet."

With Reddit, Steve and Alexis were accepted in Y Combinator's first class and given $12000 to start. They went back to Virginia, got an apartment, and started working all day and night. Still, after just two weeks, Paul sent them a scathing email and said, "Why haven't you launched your website yet? It's either because you're incapable of doing this, or you're afraid to do so, and I don't know which is worse!" Paul micromanaged them in other ways too. He hated the name and the alien that was going to be Reddit's logo. Paul said, "The alien makes you look like a joke. If you want to keep it, just put it down in the corner, so it's out of the way."

After about three weeks of intense work, Steve finished writing the code, and they got the first version of Reddit up. They decided to put parts of it online, supposing that was what Paul wanted and then sent an email to Paul saying that the basics were working. Paul, who used to write online essays, wrote his next essay and linked it to Reddit without telling them first. That essay got Reddit about a thousand visitors on its first day. Steve and Alexis hadn't planned to launch yet, as the site looked bad, but from that day forward, Reddit was launched. They started submitting content to keep their website full while working hard to get Reddit ready in time for the demo day at the end of the summer. They pitched it to a few bloggers and tried to get a little traction. Although Reddit's website was still poor quality, it started getting users, and they raised a small angel round. Reddit became the first Y Combinator company to launch.

By the end of Y Combinator's summer boot camp, Alexis and Steve had become close friends with Aron Schwartz, a Stanford dropout. Aron was also admitted to Y Combinator to work on his own startup, Infogami. Alexis, Steve, and Aron merged the Reddit and Infogami projects and pursued them together. As they began working, Reddit started really taking off, so they ended up focusing on Reddit, while Aron became an equal owner of the resulting parent company named "Not a Bug."

About three months into Reddit, Alexis got a phone call from his dad, who said his mom was in the hospital. Alexis went to see them the following day and learned that his mom had been diagnosed with terminal brain cancer. After that, Alexis felt that Reddit had to be a success to show his family that their faith in him was not wasted.

Starting from almost nothing, Reddit grew day by day into a hugely popular website. In 2006, Conde Nast Publications, the owner of Wired, approached Reddit to buy it, offering them more money for a few months of work than what their parents had made their entire lives. Steve, Alexis, and Aron sold Reddit to Conde Nast, in October of 2006, for a reported $10 million to $20 million. As soon as the acquisition was complete, Alexis called his mom and told her that her confidence in him was not wasted. Sadly, his mom passed away less than two years later.

By 2009, all three Reddit co-founders had left the company. After leaving Reddit, Alexis became a partner at Y Combinator. He also helped Steve to start a website, Hipmunk, for travel booking. In 2013, Aron Schwartz, an online icon famously known as the internet's own boy, died by suicide after being charged by federal prosecutors for violating the Computer Fraud and Abuse Act.

After five years away from the company, Steve and Alexis returned to Reddit in 2014. By that time, Reddit had become an independent company again. Alexis became executive chairman, and Steve became the company's CEO the following year. Reddit had significantly grown since they sold it in 2006, but it hadn't introduced anything new in several years. It didn't have an app and was still web-based with an outdated user interface. So, Steve and Alexis led a turnaround; as the new CEO, Steve instituted several technological improvements and launched a major redesign of Reddit's website.

When Steve and Alexis rejoined Reddit in leadership positions, one of their major plans was to launch Reddit's iOS and Android apps. Despite that, Alexis' wife Serena Williams, the renowned tennis champion, takes full credit for Reddit's app. When Alexis and Serena first met in 2015, she had no idea what Reddit was. She took out her iPhone and searched for them in the App Store but couldn't find Reddit. Serena said, "What are you talking about? There's no app in the App Store." Alexis said, "No, trust me. It's a long story, but it's going to happen, I promise!" Soon after, they launched Reddit's app.

Reddit has significantly grown since Steve and Alexis returned. As of early 2022, it is among the top twenty most-visited websites globally, and its valuation has reached more than $3 billion. Steve Huffman still runs Reddit as the CEO and plans to take the company public through an IPO.

Other than Reddit, Alexis co-founded two early-stage venture capital firms to try to be the early-stage investor he wished he had had. Alexis also wrote the best-selling book "Without Their Permission" and has been an activist for the open internet and "paid parental leave" for women and men. In the summer of 2020, Alexis Ohanian resigned as a member of Reddit's board in response to the George Floyd protests and requested to be replaced "by a Black candidate," which Reddit did.

Chapter 26

Running a Startup with Your Spouse
The Story of Robinhood's Founders

"The most valuable commodity that I know of is information."
—Gordon Gekko (Wall Street, 1987 film)

Robinhood is an American online stock brokerage known for pioneering commission-free trades of stocks, options, and cryptocurrencies, particularly popular among young people. Robinhood was founded in Palo Alto, California, in 2013 by two former Stanford roommates, Vladimir "Vlad" Tenev and Baiju Bhatt.

Vlad Tenev was born in Bulgaria during the Communist era in the late 1980s. His father was an economist and entrepreneur who had a side tourism business taking French tourists around Bulgaria and renting buses while teaching economics as a professor. His dissertation was quite Western-leaning and included many ideas from western economic books, mostly banned in communist Bulgaria. Shortly after he published his dissertation, the Berlin wall fell, and many people started coming in from the US. When a few folks from the University of Delaware came, they were intrigued to find out that there were people in Bulgaria practicing western economic theories, and Vlad's father was given the scholarship to go to the US in 1991 to continue his studies.

Vlad's father moved to the US, but Vlad and his mom remained in Bulgaria with his grandparents. Vlad could only talk to his dad once a week because the phone was very expensive. After some time, his father got an offer from the University of Maryland so his mom could move to the US too. Vlad lived with his grandparents back in Bulgaria for another six months until he joined his parents in the US. This was a defining time for his family as they had to start everything anew. None of them could speak English when they arrived in the US, which was especially difficult for Vlad, who could barely communicate with others in kindergarten.

After growing up on the East Coast, Vlad went to California to study his undergrad at Stanford, ostensibly to fulfill his dream of becoming a physicist. While doing research in the summer after his sophomore year, Vlad met Baiju, who had come to Stanford to study physics a year before him. They got along pretty well and realized they'd had similar childhoods, both having grown up in Virginia as children of immigrants. Baiju's parents had come from India to the US while his mom was pregnant with him. Since neither had any siblings, they quickly became best friends and were like brothers. They started doing problem sets and studying for midterms together and soon began working on little projects.

Vlad never thought that he could be an entrepreneur. After taking a big risk by moving to America, both his parents went to work for the same company, the world bank in Washington. They had maintained a very stable corporate lifestyle over the past twenty years. Baiju's situation was similar, but he was very interested in investing from early on. Baiju saved up a little money from his summer job at Stanford doing some research in the Physics Department. He wanted to travel to Asia, but his money wasn't enough. So, he transferred the money that he had earned to his mom and asked her to buy Apple stock for him. That was his first time getting involved with investing.

Vlad and Baiju were roommates for a couple of years. During that time, they both switched their majors from physics to math. In 2008,

Vlad finished his undergrad at Stanford, went down to Los Angeles, and started a PhD in math at UCLA to become a professor. The same year, Baiju completed his master's and took a job at a financial services company in the Bay Area. Coincidently, the financial markets collapsed during Baiju's first month working at a hedge fund and Vlad's first month in grad school.

2008 was a tumultuous year due to the financial crisis. Trading volatility went up during the big crash, in which certain automated trading strategies tended to do well. While certain parts of the financial industry felt much pain, the algorithm trading firms were fine. So many other firms realized that they had to modernize and automate their trading operations, or they might not survive the economic crisis. As a result, many firms started switching to automated trading and employed algorithms and machines instead of the old-school institutional models. Vlad and Baiju recognized a new business opportunity and decided to get into automated algorithm trading. Baiju quit his job, and Vlad dropped out of grad school. They started their company in San Francisco in 2009 and later moved to New York City to do the regularity process. They built their trading software from scratch and provided it to hedge funds and banks, most of which did not have the in-house skills to build software for automated trading. The software brought them a lot of success, and many companies bought its license.

Vlad and Baiju hired their friends from Stanford and convinced them to move across the country, but then they realized that they didn't need to be in New York as a software company. It was easier to go back to the San Francisco Bay Area and build up the team rather than talk people into moving across the country. So, they moved back to the Bay Area in late 2011, when their company was profitable and generating a few million dollars in annual revenue. The business was growing, and they could see it would reach ten million dollars a year or more over time. However, Vlad and Baiju were inspired by the Silicon Valley ecosystem to build something bigger than just enterprise software for trade optimization. They wanted to go above and beyond and create something that would affect the lives of tens of millions of people.

Vlad and Baiju noticed that most young people didn't really trust the stock market or couldn't see the value of trading. They wanted to get more people involved and help them understand how to trade and invest, but they knew that the various fees attached to trading stocks deterred young people from entering the market. So they came up with a groundbreaking idea: let people trade stocks without fees.

Having worked in finance for a few years, Baiju and Vlad realized that big Wall Street firms pay effectively nothing to trade stocks, while most people were charged a commission for every trade. Their philosophy was that everyone should have the same access to the financial markets as Wall Street insiders. They were determined to make a platform that eliminated the barriers keeping people from participating and named their new company and platform Robinhood as a symbol of freedom and justice. They hoped that Robinhood would open up trading to a new demographic by eliminating fees and streamlining the process. They also wanted Robinhood to be a modern financial adviser and spread financial information as frictionlessly as possible amongst its members.

Vlad and Baiju had this idea of making trading free, but they first would have to get registered as a broker-dealer to do that, which was a significant regulatory process. To get approved as a broker-dealer by the regulatory agencies, they had to show that they had at least one year of operating capital on hand without any revenues. It was a lot of money, and while Vlad and Baiju invested a lot of the capital from their own business to get Robinhood off the ground, they still needed more cash. However, most of the early investors were skeptical. They were concerned that Robinhood might never get the necessary approvals.

Vlad and Baiju fundraised for about five months for the seed round. They had a deadline to show they had enough capital but were still unable to meet that requirement. At one point, they thought they were on the brink of bankruptcy. As Baiju and Vlad were walking around in Palo Alto downtown hopelessly, Baiju said, "Dude, we're about to go out of business. It's been an awesome ride, but I think this is the end." About a week later, Vlad and Baiju managed to get a meeting with Tim Draper, one of the most prominent investors in Silicon Valley. Kowing that it was their last chance, they went to Tim Draper's office in San Mateo and pitched him their idea for free trading. He said, "Great idea, but you are never going to get the approval to this." Vlad and Baiju explained why they were confident that they would get the approval. He then asked, "How much are you paying yourselves, guys?" They said about $50,000 a year. He said, "You guys are paying yourself way too much. Your idea is great, but I'm out."

Vlad and Baiju left that meeting disappointed and wondering what to do. Then they got an idea. They emailed Tim Draper and agreed not to pay themselves anything until they got their brokerage license. They didn't know if they could survive that long but decided to try it regardless. They heard back from Tim, who said he was in. Baiju and Vlad started to be more frugal; they would ride a bike to work, eat cheap rice and beans, and so on. They also stopped caring if they failed because they knew they had given absolutely everything they could. Fortunately, they got their broker license about a month and a half later.

During the one year it took to get their broker-dealer license, Baiju and Vlad couldn't talk to anyone about their product; otherwise, they wouldn't get the approval. While their approval application was going in the background, they started building a mobile app with several features, including financial news, building a watchlist of stocks and rating them, upvoting news, following other investors, etc. They launched that app before being approved as a broker-dealer, planning to add trading to it later. But the app wasn't successful at all, and it turned out that having so many features was a terrible idea. Once they got their brokerage license and were able to offer the free stock trading service, only a few active users were on their app, so they shut it down and simplified their actual trading app.

When Vlad and Baiju got approval in late 2013 and were ready to announce Robinhood, they never thought it would go viral, so they planned a PR launch for the following week. Still, they wanted to test their app's popularity and decided to launch a waitlist on the Friday night before their PR. They put a simple website up and described their service as free stock trading. It was an only signup page, asking people to enter their emails to reserve a spot on the waiting list. Everyone went home after the waiting list launched. Saturday morning, Vlad woke up and checked Google analytics. He saw hundreds of people on the site simultaneously. His first thought was that there must be a bug in the system. Then he realized that someone had found their website and posted it on Reddit, and it ended up as number one in finance. A little later, he saw someone else had posted it on Hacker News. Robinhood was at number one there too. All the engineers went back to the office that Saturday to hook up emails and prepare the templates. The demand was astounding; 50,000 people signed up the first week after the announcement.

Robinhood gained a ton of momentum after it was announced. The press began writing about them, and they were able to raise more money easily. But it would be another year and a half between the announcement and when the Robinhood app fully launched to the public in March of 2015. Robinhood acquired over two million customers in their first two years, transacted over $50 billion in trading volume, and saved their customers over a half-billion dollars in trading commissions. These fees potentially would have gone to the profit of another broker.

Since its launch, Robinhood's no-commission trading model has revolutionized the brokerage industry, and gradually, most of the other brokers eliminated their trade commissions too. Over the years, Robinhood maintained its rapid growth and became the fastest-growing broker of all time. It added several new features, including a subscription model for premium accounts, crypto trading, and cash management. Trading on Robinhood increased further during the 2020 coronavirus pandemic when it attracted tens of millions of users. Robinhood became a public company in July 2021. Shortly after its IPO, Robinhood's market cap reached above $40 billion, making Vlad and Baiju billionaires.

Since co-founding Robinhood in 2012, Vlad and Baiju were both co-CEOs until November 2020, when Baiju stepped down from that position. Vlad and Baiju forged a fantastic friendship through the company, having had their desks next to each other since they started their first company together. Their friendship has been so close that they even described their Robinhood journey as "running a startup with your spouse!"

Chapter 27

Snow Devil

The Story of Shopify's Founder

"Conformity is the jailer of freedom and the enemy of growth."
—*John F. Kennedy*

Shopify is an eCommerce platform that hosts online stores and helps organize the layout of people's stores' appearance through themes. It also offers payment processing, which allows people to accept and receive payment for the products they sell. Shopify is also popular for dropshipping, which enables people to sell millions of different products without paying for inventory upfront. Tobias "Tobi" Lütke and two of his friends co-founded Shopify in 2004 in Ottawa, Canada, and launched the Shopify platform in 2006.

Tobi was born in 1982 in a middle-class family in Copelands, a tiny city in Germany. His parents bought him a computer when he was six, and he began coding at the age of eleven, spending most of his childhood programming. Coding was extremely interesting for Tobi, but it was not something that most of the other kids did back then. His town's most advanced communication method was the telephone in the early 1990s. Then the internet came there, and suddenly everyone could be connected through it, which felt super liberating to Tobi, and he also made his own website about video games.

Tobi always needed lots of money for the computers and video games he wanted because they were costly in the 90s. So, he came up with an idea to make some money to buy what he wanted. Some books had two-dimensional drawings, which you could see 3D objects hidden within the images when looked closely at. Back then, most kids loved those books, so Tobi looked them up online and found a manufacturer then called and ordered a crate of them for 80 cents per book. He sold them for ten bucks each to the students at his school and made more than enough for the computers he wanted.

Tobi was a terrible student who attended only the minimum required to pass. He was obsessed with computers and wanted to get out of school as soon as possible, so at age 16, Tobi dropped out of high school and entered an apprenticeship program to become a computer programmer. In Germany, there was an education system where someone could work for a company and apprentice under them for three years while being paid by the government. During the apprenticeship program, the student would usually spend one day a week in school and the rest at the company, which was the perfect situation for Tobi. He apprenticed as a computer programmer for Siemens, which allowed him to spend his entire day doing what he loved.

The 90s was the peak of United States mania in Germany. Tobi thought that all the best modern technologies came from the United States and wanted to move there at some point. He figured that Canada was close to the United States, and he could find a way from there to America. So, in 2002, at the age of 22, Tobi went to Canada. The winters were much longer than what Tobi used to in Germany, so he spent a lot of time snowboarding. While snowboarding in a resort in British Columbia, he met his future girlfriend and wife, Fiona McCain. Fiona was from Ottawa, so Tobi moved there to be with her.

Tobi wanted to work as a computer programmer in Canada, but he did not have a work permit yet. Fortunately, he learned that he did not need a work permit to start his own business because he was not technically working until he began earning money. Tobi and some of his friends had many snowboards, so they decided to start a business to sell them. Since Tobi had a background in programming, they decided to start with an online store first and open a physical store later after generating some income. Tobi assumed setting up the online store would be the most minor problem of starting their business, but it turned out to be an exercise in pure frustration for him. He first tried to build their online store using existing software and signed up for every piece available. There was some software for online shopping carts, but it was designed for existing businesses. In 2004, there was no software to specifically support people who wanted to start new companies online. Eventually, Tobi decided enough was enough; he started coding software to run their store the way he wanted.

After building the software from scratch, Tobi and his friends opened an online store called "Snow Devil" and started selling snowboards. It was around the time the dot-com crash hit Canada, and there were not many competitions online. During that time, Tobi advertised his snowboards on Google. An ad for his business appeared when searching the names of all the ski resorts in Canada. Because of this savvy marketing, he sold a lot of snowboards that winter. Yet after a successful season, people stopped buying snowboards when summer came. By then, however, a few people had asked Tobi if they could license the software he wrote. The idea of Shopify came from those people who wanted to use Tobi's software to start an online business. Tobi co-founded Shopify with two of his friends in 2004, but they spent another two years working on it before he finally launched Shopify in 2006.

Tobi realized that they needed some help and hired some staff, but it was tough to get any investments initially. He took a lot of money from his family to start the company, but it didn't come together right away, and they were running out of money. He knew the software was good, but he didn't know how to get people to use it. Tobi didn't earn any salary for the first three and a half years, so he and his wife moved in with his in-laws to save money. His father-in-law was the only person who remained solvent enough to put more money into the company, carrying Shopify's payroll for about a year by himself. But even when they only had enough money for a few weeks left in the bank, Tobi insisted that his team make plans about products they needed a year later.

In the beginning, if someone wanted Shopify software, they had to talk to salespeople as there were no prices on the website. Then they tried a freemium model for about a year: no money upfront and then charging a percentage-based fee. This turned out to cost nothing for people who didn't have any sales and way too much for people who had good sales. Shopify then changed to a subscription model, letting people start their online stores at an affordable price.

Shopify revolutionized eCommerce for new businesses by helping them build an online presence with a few clicks and a credit card. After a rough start, Shopify gradually started growing and becoming successful. Today, Shopify is one of the most popular eCommerce platforms on the planet. In a 2020 press release, Shopify announced that their platform powered over one million businesses in more than 175 countries across the globe.

Tobi has served as the Shopify CEO since 2008. According to Forbes, he owns nearly 7% of the company, which went public through an IPO in 2015. In its debut on the New York Stock Exchange, Shopify started trading at $28 per share. As of early 2022, Shopify's share price has risen to about $1000, giving the company a market cap value of more than $120 billion and placing Tobi Lütke among the top billionaires in the world.

Chapter 28

Epic Food Poisoning

The Story of Slack's Founders

"We are what we repeatedly do. Excellence, then, is not an act, but a habit."
—*Aristotle*

Slack is a communication platform and collaboration hub that many businesses use to connect with their staff. It includes instant messaging, voice and video calls, and a suite of tools to help groups share information and work together. Users can also upload and share files and integrate Slack with other apps and services. Slack was started by Stewart Butterfield in 2013 in Vancouver, Canada.

Stewart Butterfield was born to hippy parents in a little town called Lund in British Colombia, Canada. His father was from New York and had fled the US to avoid being drafted for the Vietnam War. Stewart grew up in a log cabin with no electricity and running water with parents who did things like grow weed in a rain forest or raise pigs. When Stewart was five, they moved to the city so he could go to school. His father got a job in real estate business development, and throughout his childhood, Stewart witnessed several businesses started by his dad.

In his second grade, Stewart became fascinated by computers and started learning to program. He began with a multi-media presentation of the world flags and some simple games at school. Then he got an Apple computer at home, and a copy of a magazine called Bite, which had a couple of pages of programs that someone could just type out in an Apple, change a couple of things, and see what happened. But as Stewart grew up, computers became less and less interesting to him throughout high school.

Stewart began college in 1992 and discovered the internet on his school's Unix machine about a year before it became widely popular. It was a mind-blowing experience for Stewart, who was fascinated with the idea that people could find their community irrespective of what that community was. Many of his friends went to universities in different cities, so he used email to talk to them. Back then, HTML, the web code, was very simple. So Stewart taught it to himself. In 1993, he was one of five people in his hometown who knew HTML. For the next few years, his job during school and summers was making websites for people.

Stewart really wanted a degree in cognitive science, but the school he went to didn't have that option. Cognitive science was a combination of computer science, psychology, linguistics, and philosophy, all courses he wanted to take. However, there were many requirements for every class in psychology, whereas it was a pretty light set of requirements in philosophy, so Stewart chose that. He received his BA in philosophy from the University of Victoria in 1996 and earned a Master of Philosophy from Cambridge in 1998. Afterward, Stewart planned to complete his PhD. One of his friends had finished his PhD and gotten a job at the University of Lowville in Kentucky. But his friend didn't really want to live in Lowville and felt his job was terrible because of the low pay. Meanwhile, some of his friends had moved to the San Francisco Bay Area, and they were making twice as much money as him, having fun, and working on new stuff. It was right around the beginning of the dot-com era. Since Stewart was good at HTML, he decided to work on the internet instead of doing a PhD.

After getting two degrees in philosophy, Stewart became a web developer. He went back to British Colombia in 1999 and designed the web page of the biggest design agency there. He didn't really know anything about design, but he eventually became the head of the design group anyway. The owner had started the company in 1993 and had registered tons of domain names like keyboard.com, brazil.com, makeup.com, etc. A few years later, those domain names had become significant assets.

After working at the company for some time, Stewart began thinking about starting his own business. Since discovering the internet, Stewart had become very interested in online social interactions. By 2000, people had started developing personas and interacting with other people over the internet in different virtual communities and blogs. Personally, Stewart had the experience of having a crush on someone that he had never actually met. He fell in love with her online persona and the things she said in the comments. After considering different ideas, Stewart decided to create a game as a pretext for social interaction, and he and some of his friends started a company in the spring of 2002. This was right after the dot-com crash and 9/11, a terrible time for financial markets. The tech-heavy Nasdaq was down more than eighty percent from its peak, and no one wanted to invest in internet companies anymore. They raised a little bit of money from their friends and family and spent about a year building a prototype, which became very popular among the small group of people who developed it. But it took them another year and a half to fully finish it, and by then, they couldn't raise any more money. At one point, the one person on the team who had kids was the only person that was getting paid.

The idea of a game that played as a pretext for social interactions seemed really interesting, but it turned out to be a terrible idea, commercially. So, after failing to find a large audience for their game, they decided to find another use for the technology they had developed. While still looking for new ideas, Stewart flew to New York City from Vancouver for a conference. He got food poisoning on the flight and started puking in the immigration hall at JFK airport, and kept vomiting all the way to his hotel. That night, after being awake feverish and frantic, Stewart came up with a new idea in his hallucinations: making a photo-sharing platform. He wrote out the whole first version of what would become Flickr and how it would take advantage of their technologies around three in the morning.

Digital cameras had just started to become common in 2003. Around the same time, the very first camera phones came out, and the internet was getting fast enough to view photos. These things were all happening simultaneously, but there was no functional online platform for sharing photos at the time. So, the idea of a photo-sharing website seemed very promising to Stewart and his co-founders. They had developed a game client with a messaging server on the back-end, and it was possible to repurpose it to make a photo-sharing client. For them, Flickr was a last-ditch attempt to make something out of the technology they had already developed. They started developing Flickr in 2003 and launched it in 2004. Stewart's idea was that Flickr could be photography as a pretext for social interaction similar to their game. People could put a photo online for others to see and comment on it. These images could also have a title and description, and people could tag them and create groups. It was like a social network that revolved around photographs, starting right around the same time as Facebook did.

Flickr was a big success and quickly became so popular that by 2005 Yahoo wanted to buy it. So, Stewart and his co-founders sold Flickr to Yahoo for twenty-five million dollars, which was a lot of money at the time. The Flickr team joined Yahoo after the acquisition. Stewart hadn't ever worked inside of a big company before. For him, it was tough coming from a nine-person company where he could decide something in the morning, code it, and then release it in the afternoon to a long cycle of decision-making, which Yahoo was well known for. Stewart found working in that environment very frustrating and finally left Yahoo in 2008.

After leaving Yahoo, Stewart went up to Vancouver to start

another gaming company called Glitch. He and three other people who were on the original team at Flickr and had worked together at Yahoo decided to make the same game in 2009 that they were trying to make in 2002. They thought many things had changed from 2002 to 2009: more people were online, computers were faster, people had high-speed internet, and smartphones were capable of internet access. Besides, Stewart and his team were much more experienced, so it was much easier for them to raise money. Everything seemed to be ready for them to become successful this time. Except, their idea was still not very commercially viable. Glitch was a web-based, massively multiplayer game, but it was very complicated; even explaining what it was to someone new could take several minutes.

They started developing Glitch using flash as the front-end technology right when that technology was about to die. Besides that, people were also switching from desktop to mobile after the first iPhone came out in 2008. After working for two years on Glitch, Stewart realized that they had to shut down that game again and think of something else. They had gotten $17 million in venture capital money and had spent about $12 million by then. With $5 million left in the bank, they called their investors and said, "This game isn't working. We're going to give you back the rest of your money." However, none of their investors wanted their money back. Instead, they asked Stewart to try something else.

Glitch founders argued about what they wanted to do next for an extended period. While working on their game, they had used an old technology called Internet Relay Chat or IRC. After starting to use IRC, they realized that it had many deficiencies, including being unable to store and forward messages. If someone wanted to send a message to a person who was not online at that moment, the message would be lost. So, they built a system to log the messages and store them in an archive. Once they had the messages in a database, they wanted to be able to search them. So, they built a search on top of that. Then feature by feature, they created things to integrate with their file server and slowly developed a system that became the foundation of all company communications. Their internally-built communication system turned out to be really useful for many reasons. It provided transparency across the organization, and everyone could see what others were talking about. The engineers could see the conversations of the designers, and the issues of the customer supports were visible to everyone. Another big advantage was when they hired people, the new hires had access to the whole archive. They could just open up different company channels and scroll back to see the previous chats. Stewart and other Glitch co-founders thought that other software developer teams would probably like such a system as well. So, they decided that was what they would do instead of Glitch. They set up a partner meeting and presented their new big idea called Slack to their investors; they liked it.

When they decided to switch to Slack, Glitch had around 45 employees, including animators, musicians, writers, illustrators, and many people whose skills were not transferrable to Slack. They had to lay off most of their team. Stewart called an all-hands meeting to make the announcement internally and got up in front of the whole company. As soon as he started talking, he locked eyes with one of their employees who had just had started three months before. Stewart himself had convinced him to move to a new city with his wife and two-year-old daughter. He had bought a new house there and moved away from his in-laws, who were helping take care of the kids. It was heartbreaking for Stewart to tell him that he didn't have a job anymore, but he had to lay off 37 people despite feeling terrible about it.

Stewart and his team started developing Slack, and two months later, the first version was ready to be used by themselves. A couple of months later, they decided to get some people to try the Slack prototype and tell them what they thought. But they had a real problem convincing their friends and other people at different companies to try it. Slack was a product that, at the time, no companies knew they needed, and using it wasn't a decision that one person could make; a whole group had to agree. Although it was very hard to convince anyone to initially try Slack, once they started trying it, they stuck with it. Stewart and his team had put a lot of effort into the user experience. As a result, Slack was very user-friendly and felt chitty-chatty with users. It felt more like a consumer app than enterprise software.

Slack reached a billion-dollar valuation at the record-setting pace of eight months, and was released to the public in 2014. Thousands of customers signed up for the service within hours of its launch. Slack's popularity grew very quickly, and in late 2015, it passed more than a million daily active users. Slack was an innovative idea that transformed the way organizations communicate and had limited competitors from 2014 to 2017. In 2017, however, Microsoft launched its Teams app. Despite that, Slack remained popular and continued to grow. In June 2019, Slack went public through a direct public offering, reaching a market value of about $20 billion. At the time it filed to go public, Slack reported it had millions of daily active users from more than 150 countries. Once again, there was a buyer for the company that Stewart created. Salesforce, the giant enterprise software company, acquired Slack for approximately $28 billion in July 2021.

Chapter 29

Peekaboo

The Story of Snapchat's Founders

"Design is not just what it looks like and feels like. Design is how it works."
—*Steve Jobs*

S napchat is an image and video messaging app with disappearing posts, or stories, which are wildly popular with teenagers. The company also develops and manufactures the wearable camera Spectacles, smart glasses that connect to the user's Snapchat account and record videos. Snapchat was created by Stanford University students Evan Spiegel and Bobby Murphy in 2011.

Evan was born in 1990 and grew up near Los Angeles. He got his first Macintosh when he was a kid. Being able to change things quickly with computers amazed him from a young age. Evan was nerdy and shy who was often bullied when he was in school. His parents didn't let him watch tv growing up, so it was harder for him to relate to other kids. He also didn't like sports, preferring to spend time on the computer and read. That experience at a young age gave him the confidence to go his own path and not worry so much about what other people thought of him. Evan's best friends in middle and high school were his computer teachers. His computer teacher in high school helped him build his own personal computer by the time he was in sixth grade. Around that time, Evan also learned about graphic design, which became his new passion.

A few years later, Evan went to study product design at Stanford University. While there, a family friend let him sit in a graduate-level class on entrepreneurship and venture capital, where he heard talks from some of the most successful people in tech. Evan became friends with Intuit co-founder Scott Cook after he gave a talk at one of those classes and asked him for a job. Cook let Evan work on a product Intuit planned to release in India. After gaining valuable experience there, Evan decided to work on his own ideas.

Just as Evan started thinking about working on his own project, he met Bobby Murphy, a mathematics and computer science student at Stanford in his fraternity. Bobby's background in computers and Evan's background in design were a good match. They decided to work with each other and tried several projects, including a website named Future Freshmen, which they built to help high school students apply to college. They spent about a year and a half and some money on it, but their website didn't take off after putting in all those hours. Evan and Bobby had two siblings that were applying to college at the time, and neither of them would use Future Freshmen. They thought if even their family wouldn't use their website, no one would.

Evan and Bobby realized that they loved working together despite their failed projects. They kept exploring new ideas until the concept for Snapchat came in spring 2011. They noticed there was a lot of pressure on social media because everything posted there would last forever. Evan and Bobby thought, "What if you could send photos that disappear? It'd be fun to be able to send pictures back and forth with your friends and not worry about them." They also thought that deleting images after sending them would mean taking a picture wasn't about saving an important moment anymore, but about communicating. The widespread use of smartphones with cameras and connections to the internet made using photos for communication seem even more intuitive.

In the summer of 2011, Evan and Bobby stayed at Evan's dad's house to work on their project. From building Future Freshmen, they had learned that rather than spending all their time making the perfect product, they should try to make something simple and see if people liked it. So they built a small prototype of an app called Picaboo for sending pictures that would disappear after a set amount of time. Evan focused on designing the user interface while Bobby did the coding.

Evan and Bobby launched their app in July 2011 and started using it with their friends and family, but they still needed more users to determine whether the app was good or not. There was an outdoor mall near Evan's father's house, so Evan made some flyers, went to that mall, and walked up to people and said, "Hey, would you like to send a disappearing picture?" Although most people said no, they got their first five hundred customers by doing that. After some time, their app started spreading by word-of-mouth as teenagers started chatting on it one by one and inviting their friends to join. As Evan and Bobby supposed, many people loved their app because they could communicate visually, which felt more expressive than text. Later that year, they changed their app's name from Picaboo to Snapchat. Downloads started to spike in January 2012, and by February, Snapchat had tens of thousands of users.

As Snapchat's users grew, Evan and Bobby were maxing out their credit cards on the servers, paying a couple of thousand dollars a month. Fundraising was tough, as investors didn't believe that sending disappearing pictures could be a really big idea or successful business. Using images to communicate was hard to explain to most people who never used Snapchat. So, Evan started borrowing money from his dad, promising he would make enough money to pay for the server bills themselves one day. But that day was taking a long time to arrive, and Evan's dad finally was tired of waiting and said, "I'm not paying for people to send disappearing photos anymore."

Finally, they got a break. An investor from Silicon Valley whose kids used Snapchat and had heard its popularity among teenagers reached out to Evan and asked to meet. It turned out Evan and Bobby had been fortunate because their business had been growing over about a year before they took any funding, and more importantly, people who started using Snapchat didn't stop using it during that time. Some other apps were very popular, and people would download and play them for a week or a month and then stop. But once people started using Snapchat, they used it all the time. Based on those facts, their investor decided to invest half a million dollars in Snapchat.

Evan was in a CNC machining class at Stanford, waiting to finally get their first investment in Snapchat. He was sitting in the back of the class, constantly refreshing his bank account to see when the half a million dollars hit their bank account. When it did, he went up to the professor and said, "I'm so sorry, but I have to drop this class because I really need to focus full-time on my business." Evan dropped out of Stanford in 2012, just a few credits short of graduation, to work on Snapchat full-time.

Although he didn't earn his diploma, Evan was allowed to walk across the stage to collect it with his classmates. Stanford lets its students walk through graduation even if they haven't finished the requirements necessary to get their diploma. The University created this program for students using the summer to finish up their degrees. But Evan was embarrassed and didn't want to be left out of the celebration. On the stage, they handed him an empty folder as he waved to his family, who had traveled all the way to Stanford to watch him.

After dropping out of Stanford, Evan focused entirely on Snapchat, which was growing rapidly. As Evan and Bobby raised more money and built their company, they managed to retain the majority voting control. That meant that they could fail, but no one was able to fire them, which gave them the opportunity to learn from their mistakes and continue.

By the middle of 2013, Snapchat had more than fifty million downloads. Soon, other companies wanted to buy Snapchat, but Evan and Bobby didn't want to sell their company. They rejected a $3 billion offer from Facebook CEO Mark Zuckerberg in 2013 and then turned down a subsequent $4 billion offer from Google. People thought of them as crazy and arrogant when they decided not to sell their company even when it wasn't making any money. But Evan and Bobby kept focusing on making Snapchat better, and a few years later, their company went public in 2017 at a valuation of roughly $33 billion, making them instant billionaires.

Over the years, Snapchat kept adding new features. Some of them became so popular that other social media platforms copied them. The company also expanded its offerings beyond the Snapchat app and unveiled smart sunglasses with a built-in camera called Spectacles. The Snap augmented reality lenses and filters helped with popularizing video messaging. As of early 2022, hundreds of million people use Snapchat daily.

Evan's wife, the Australian supermodel Miranda Kerr, is also an entrepreneur, and neither of them had a college degree. After their son was born in 2018, Evan imagined having a conversation with his child when he was a teenager and thinking about college. Evan thought his son would ask, "Dad, you and mom never graduated from college. Why do I need to go to college?" Evan didn't want to get into that debate with their son, so he decided to go back to college and finish his education. He returned to Stanford and took the same CNC machining class taught by the same professor. Evan Spiegel graduated from Stanford with a BS in product design in 2018, six years after he dropped out.

Chapter 30

A Little Too Naïve

The Story of Spotify's Founders

"When you go fishing, you can catch a lot of fish, or you can catch a big fish."
—*Sean Parker (The Social Network, 2010 film)*

S potify is a digital music streaming service that gives people access to millions of songs, podcasts, and videos from artists worldwide for free. Affordable premium plans are also available for people who want to listen to ad-free music. Music can be streamed via the internet through a mobile phone or a computer without downloading tracks. Daniel Ek and Martin Lorentzon founded Spotify in 2006 in Stockholm, Sweden.

Daniel Ek was born in 1983 in Stockholm, Sweden, and grew up there with a single mom. She worked at a care center, so they didn't have much money. When Daniel was 4 years old, his family wanted him to play an instrument, so they gave him a guitar. About a year later, Daniel got his first computer: a Commodore VIC-20. It was one of the earliest versions of home computers, so Daniel found it boring, but a year later, he got a Commodore 64, which had 200 games. Eventually, he grew bored of all the games, but sometime later, he found a programming book and started reading it. The first example in the book was how to write a game, so Daniel decided to try to write his own game. Daniel asked a family friend what the hardest thing you could learn in computers was and that person said C++ was really difficult because it would take 40 pages of code just to get something simple done. He decided to learn it because it seemed challenging.

As Daniel started learning to program, he got more familiar with the internet and the online world. Sweden got high-speed internet in 1998, so he could search for anything online, and soon, Daniel also learned how to make websites. In Sweden, most of the firms creating sites charged about fifty grand for a simple two-page website. Local people, who couldn't afford such a high price, began asking Daniel to help them make their homepages. When the first person asked him to make one, Daniel said he would do it for a hundred bucks to see if he could. The person said yes. So, Daniel made the website. Next time, another person came and asked if he could create one for them. This time Daniel asked for $200, and again the person said OK. It kept evolving until he was charging $5000 per homepage!

While still in elementary school, Daniel already had so many people knocking at his door asking him to create websites for them that he couldn't do it by himself anymore. He figured there had to be some correlation between math and programming, so he taught his classmates and friends who were good at math to program HTML. And then, because he figured out that he wasn't that good at design, he started teaching photoshop to the students who were good at drawing, and his teachers let him use school equipment to do all this. He realized that things like games and cell phones were more valuable than cash for kids, so he bribed them to help him with the work. Eventually, he had the whole class working on projects and building web pages after school.

Daniel and his family were living in a pretty rough neighborhood at the time, but Daniel was making almost sixty thousand a month. No one in his family even knew he was working on his business. They thought that it was just a hobby, and when he started buying really expensive guitars, his family didn't understand their values. Then a huge TV entered their house. They called his teachers and asked what he was actually up to. The teachers thought he was just teaching people photoshop and HTML, so they said, "He is a good student and is educating all other kids." By this time, Daniel was bribing his classmates to do his homework or sometimes even to take his exams.

By 14, Daniel had started his first company making websites. After that, he built a few other companies for web hosting and web design. In 1999, Daniel discovered Google and was amazed by it. He was very interested in the technology, so he applied for Google, but Google turned him down because he didn't have a university degree. Irritated at Google, Daniel decided to make his own search engine thinking it couldn't be that hard. He took money from his web design company and poured it into making a search engine but lost it all. It turned out making a good search engine like Google was actually quite difficult. But he was still naïve enough to believe that things would work out somehow and didn't fully understand how hard certain things were, so he was open to pursuing impossible dreams.

After failing to make a search engine, Daniel built a business for search engine optimization and marketing. He was spending all the money they were making buying servers, hiring programmers, and playing with exciting projects without knowing what exactly to do with them. He had also built all these companies without keeping track of paying taxes. One day, when he was about 19 years old, Daniel got a letter from the Swedish IRS saying that he owed them a couple of hundred thousand dollars in taxes. He had no idea how to pay for that, so he decided to go into personal bankruptcy, which was particularly tough because he had thirty employees at the time doing projects for him and he had to lay off them.

Things changed in 2005 when Skype was sold to eBay. The market suddenly opened up, and other companies started looking to acquire as eBay did. Daniel sold four companies and went from bankruptcy to having a few million dollars in the bank in just a couple of months, becoming a millionaire when he was only 22 years old. Daniel thought everything would be much better with money, but it turned out the money wasn't very helpful. After buying a lot of stuff, he started thinking about what else to do. He partied for a while, trying to meet women, but he wasn't that successful. He got really depressed. All he wanted was to be accepted and really to belong. However, he realized that money did not matter, and it certainly didn't make him happier.

Daniel started thinking about what truly mattered to him. He realized that he had fun with all his companies, but they never felt like he belonged. He had co-founded and was the CTO of Stardoll, a website for young girls to dress up virtual paper dolls, which had more than 100 million registered users, playing with those dolls and sharing them. But Daniel didn't want to stay with Stardoll. He knew that people liked it, but it wasn't his passion. So, he asked himself, "If I want to spend five years of my life on just one thing, what would that be?" It was obvious to him that he wanted to focus on music. He also wanted the problem to be big enough to have a potential impact that would change the entire world.

In 2006, there were some peer-to-peer file-sharing websites like Napster that people used illegally to share music so others could download it for free. Daniel believed that laws could never prevent music piracy; laws could help, but they would never solve the problem completely. Only creating a better service than piracy and, at the same time, compensating the music industry could do that. That gave him the idea of Spotify: making millions of songs available to people for free! It was an absolutely crazy idea at that time. Daniel decided to start Spotify with one of his friends, Martin Lorentzon. Daniel and Martin became friends when Martin's company acquired one of Daniel's previous online advertising firms.

Daniel and Martin's initial vision was to let people have all the world's music in their music libraries. Many entrepreneurs had tried that before and invested hundreds of millions of dollars, but they all failed. Most of them had been sued for billions of dollars. When Daniel decided to get into the music industry, everyone told him he was crazy because he didn't know how hard it would be to do a music startup. But he was 23 at the time and had built successful companies before, so again he thought it couldn't be that hard. Even though

Daniel and Martin initially wanted to make all music free, they wondered how they could make money from a free product. So they decided to try audio advertising. Most investors, however, believed there was no market for audio advertisement, and it wasn't going to work. But Daniel and Martin believed in it so much that they put in $10 million of their own money to start their company.

When starting Spotify, Daniel didn't know what was involved in getting licenses from record labels. He and Martin thought it would take them about six months to get the required licensing. Their logic was that the music business was going downhill, so those companies would want to get the music out there to as many people as possible. They also thought they would figure out how to deal with its cost later once they get the scale. To make the deals with record labels, Daniel was introduced to someone in the music industry. Daniel asked him for help, but he was told it wouldn't be as easy as he thought because he needed to make deals with people individually. Still, he promised to introduce him to those people, so Daniel went to New York and sat down with all the major labels. Initially, everyone seemed supportive of his idea; they told him, "This seems interesting. We'll try to figure something out if you can come back in a few weeks." He walked out, called his co-founder Martin, and said, "They seemed totally reasonable. We should be able to launch it in about six months." Yet it took them two and half years because, after their initial discussions, the companies did a 180 and told him, "No, this isn't going to happen. Don't come back!" Daniel called Martin up again and told him about the situation. Martin said, "That's totally fine. If that's the case, let's do something else. Just give it another couple of weeks, and then we'll figure it out." Reassured by his co-founder, Daniel canceled his trip back home to Stockholm and instead started camping out in front of the label companies' offices like a homeless person for about two months to get the meeting he wanted. And he met everyone, from the janitors to the CEOs.

Their initial plan for Spotify was to launch it worldwide on day one. However, after the pushbacks, they decided not to go to the US and instead to start in a territory that didn't matter as much to those companies. Daniel wanted to prove the model first. That decision saved Spotify, and everything turned around. He finally got the deals after two and half years. Spotify was launched in Europe at the end of 2008, during the financial crisis in the United States. Daniel and Martin wanted to expand from Europe very soon. However, it took them another three years to convince the media companies that letting Spotify operate in the US was the right move.

Under Daniel's leadership as the company's CEO, Spotify gained worldwide popularity very fast and today it is the world's largest music streaming service provider, surpassing competitors like Apple and Amazon music. As of 2022, Spotify has hundreds of millions of monthly active users, including more than 160 million paying subscribers. Spotify listed its shares on the New York Stock Exchange in April 2018 in an unusual direct listing without the help of investment banks, and by 2021, Spotify's market value soared to more than $40 billion. According to Forbes, Daniel Ek owns nearly 9% of the Spotify shares, making him a young billionaire.

Chapter 31

Man in Black

The Story of Telegram's Founder

"I don't like the idea that I'm not in control of my life."
—Neo (The Matrix, 1999 film)

Telegram is an online messaging app that works like popular messaging apps WhatsApp and Facebook Messenger. It is cloud-based and focuses on security and speed. Telegram was founded in 2013 by Pavel Durov, the same person who created the popular social media platform VKontakte, more commonly known as VK.

Pavel Durov was born in 1984 in Saint Petersburg, Russia. For much of his childhood, he lived in Turin, Italy, where his father, a renowned Russian scholar, worked for many years. Pavel and his older brother Nikolai learned how to code in school, and Nikolai was so good at coding that he became a world champion programmer twice as a student.

At the age of 17, Pavel and his family moved back to Russia, where Pavel followed in his father's footsteps and attended the Philological Department of Saint Petersburg State University. While studying, he created an online library for his fellow students to share books and notes. Pavel's website became popular all over the university and encouraged him to launch a university forum in 2006. A newspaper in Saint Petersburg noticed Pavel's university forum and published an article about it. Pavel's former classmate who had studied in America and used Facebook came across the article. He contacted Pavel and showed him Facebook for the first time. Talking to his old classmate inspired Pavel to create a similar platform for Russian users to find former schoolmates and lost childhood friends. With his genius brother Nikolai's help, and funds from his father, Pavel launched the beta version of his social network website VKontakte, shortly known as VK, in November 2006.

VK was initially supposed to be a network for students. Soon, however, the students' siblings, parents, and even grandparents joined the website. VK grew quickly, reaching over 100,000 users at the beginning of 2007 and one million members by July of the same year. People liked its friendly interface and the variety of games and applications. It quickly became the most visited website in Russia and one of the largest social networks in Europe.

As VK gained popularity, it caught the attention of some political readers. Between 2011 and 2013, VK reportedly was used as a hub by anti-government protestors who organized events. A formal request was sent to Pavel, asking him to block all political opposition accounts on VK. Despite the pressure, Pavel refused to comply with the request. Instead, he posted a picture of a dog in a hoodie with its tongue sticking out on his VK and Twitter pages, calling it his response to the request. But the Russian government did not think that was funny and soon sent a SWAT team to raid his apartment. The raid was abandoned when Pavel refused to answer the door. However, Pavel's troubles didn't end there. The Russian government launched an intense smear campaign against Pavel. In 2013, when Pavel was 28, he was investigated for an alleged hit-and-run incident. He was accused of being the driver of a white Mercedes, even though he didn't own a car or know how to drive. Meanwhile, shares of his company were being bought out by pro-Kremlin investors. He gradually lost control of VK and was forced out of the company in 2014. Pavel sold his 12% stake for around $300 million dollars even though it was worth billions of dollars. He took that money with him and fled Russia.

Pavel didn't know where to go after his self-imposed exile, but he had a lot of cash and sought new citizenship. He found it on Saint Kitts and Nevis, an island country in the Caribbean where he was granted citizenship following a $250,000 donation to their sugar industry diversification foundation.

When Pavel's house was surrounded by a SWAT team, all he wanted to do was to call his brother. But there was no form of communication that was totally secure from government surveillance. In the middle of that tense situation, he was inspired by the idea of a secure messenger. After being forced to leave Russia and his company behind, Pavel immediately started working on his next idea: a messenger app for fully encrypted messaging and communication.

Once again, with the help of his brother Nikolai, Pavel created and launched a messenger app called Telegram, which they paid to develop with their own money. Telegram allowed users to send messages and media on a completely secure platform using end-to-end encryption technology. Without any marketing, millions of people started using it, and Telegram reached one billion messages sent daily by the end of 2014. Since then, Telegram has been competing with messaging apps like WhatsApp and Facebook messenger and has reached the milestone of 500 million users worldwide in 2021.

Pavel has made Telegram free to use and spends his own money to keep it running. According to Forbes, owning the majority of Telegram puts Pavel among the top billionaires of 2022. After leaving Russia, Pavel, who always dresses in all black resembling Neo from "Matrix" movies, traveled around the world until he settled in Dubai, where the Telegram's operation is now located.

Chapter 32

Heavy Information Consumer
The Story of TikTok's Founder

"Change before you have to."
—*Jack Welch*

TikTok is one the fastest growing social media worldwide. It allows users to create, watch, and share short videos shot on mobile devices. With its personalized feeds of quirky videos set to music and sound effects, the app is notable for its addictive quality and high levels of engagement. TikTok and its parent company ByteDance were created by the Chinese entrepreneur Zhang Yiming.

Zhang was born in Fujian, China, in 1983. His home province was among the earliest regions in the Chinese mainland to open up to the world. Zhang's passion for the business was inspired by his parents, who had started their own electronics-related business when he was young. Zhang had been a great consumer of information since his childhood, reading a lot of newspapers and magazines when he was in middle school, cover to cover. At that time, people believed that biology would spearhead the 21st century, and Zhang was interested in it. When he was in high school, he read a book called "General

Biology," which influenced him greatly. In 2001 he enrolled at Nankai University in Tianjin to study as a biology major. But when he entered the school, he first transferred to the microelectronics major and later transferred to software engineering because he thought there were only a few opportunities for experimentation in microelectronics. He wanted hands-on experience and quick results.

There were not many extracurricular activities in Tianjin, so Zhang had a lot of time to read a wide assortment of books, and biographies accounted for a large part of them. One of his favorites was Jack Welch's - former CEO of GE - biography. In his college days, Zhang also built websites and troubleshot computer problems for extra money. Zhang met his wife in university while helping to fix her computer, and he continued repairing her computer until she agreed to date him.

In 2005, Zhang graduated from Nankai University and went to Beijing to work for Kuxun, an online travel booking startup. He was one of the first employees and started as an ordinary engineer at the beginning. But a year later, he was promoted to a technical director, where he was in charge of about fifty people working on the back-end technology. Zhang left his startup job in 2008 to work for Microsoft because he wanted to know how corporations manage their businesses. However, he soon felt suffocated by the company's corporate rules and left to join another startup named Fanfou, a Chinese microblogging website similar to Twitter, which failed a couple years later.

Zhang's experience working on social media gave him the opportunity to observe users' behavior. He noticed that the wave of mobile internet would be very large, and many users were migrating from computers to smartphones. Zhang left Fanfou in 2009 and took over Kuxun's real estate search business. He then started his first company called 99fang and began developing mobile apps for real estate. In six months, he launched several mobile applications, which soon became the most popular real estate apps in China.

99fang was doing fine, but Zhang started thinking about going in a new direction. He was obsessed with information circulation since he was a child and wanted to make a platform that would distribute information based on personal interests rather than search engine results mixed with advertisements and non-relevant content. He quit his position at 99fang to focus on building his new venture and founded ByteDance in his apartment in Beijing in 2012. His new company had a humble start; he bought all their furniture from IKEA, and their meeting room was only about five square feet. Zhang once saw a slogan at a construction site near his apartment that read, "small place, big dream." Inspired by that slogan, he envisioned making a global company from that small apartment.

When Zhang first founded ByteDance, investors doubted the 29-year-old and his ideas. Back then, most venture capitalists in China did not believe in artificial intelligence, so he couldn't raise any capital. Finally, an international company agreed to invest some money in the startup, and with the funding, Zhang launched the news aggregator app Toutiao in August 2012. Toutiao used artificial intelligence to analyze user preferences through their social media accounts and then deliver customized news, so people only received news that they cared about. Toutiao quickly became popular in China. Within two years, the app had attracted more than thirteen million daily users. That number grew to more than a hundred million by the fall of 2014. But not everybody was happy with Toutiao, especially traditional media outlets who felt their original content was stolen by the news aggregator. After a flurry of copyright lawsuits, Zhang tweaked Touiao's systems and negotiated deals with newspapers and other media partners to share revenue.

In 2014, Zhang visited Silicon Valley for the first time to present about artificial intelligence at Facebook's headquarter in California. During his visit, Zhang noticed that Snapchat was gaining popularity among teenagers in the US. He wanted to engage with the young people as well and began to develop a video-sharing app where users could create short lip sync comedy and talent videos. He integrated artificial intelligence to recommend similar content to the users based on their preferences and searches. The app, named Douyin, was developed in less than a year and launched in China in 2016. Douyin became an instant hit and got 100 million users within a year, with more than one billion videos viewed every day.

Seeing the great response for Douyin, Zhang built a global version of the app named TikTok. Within two months of TikTok's launch in 2017, ByteDance had spent around $1 billion to purchase the karaoke-style video app Musical.ly. Musical.ly was already very popular with teens and younger millennials in the US, and when Musical.ly merged with TikTok, it provided a substantial user base in the US. TikTok kept both apps' core features: short-form videos, and suddenly became a global internet sensation. Within a year, TikTok became the third most downloaded non-game app globally, following behind WhatsApp and Facebook messenger.

Since its launch in 2016, TikTok has become a cultural phenomenon worldwide. However, it has faced challenges caused by regulatory issues at home and abroad while trying to keep its momentum. In 2020, over concerns that the app posed a national security risk, the US administration gave TikTok the executive ultimatum to be sold to an American company or be banned from the country. Despite the controversies, TikTok managed to stave off a ban and remains one of the most popular social networks among American teens.

TikTok hit two billion downloads in 2020, surpassing Facebook, Instagram, and YouTube to become the world's most downloaded iOS app. TikTok's parent company ByteDance is worth $250 billion as of 2022, making it the most valuable privately held company globally, according to Bloomberg. Zhang owns roughly a quarter of Byte-Dance, putting him among China and the world's richest people. At just 38 years old, Zhang announced in May 2021 that he would step down as CEO and transition to a new role to focus on long-term strategy. In his announcement letter to ByteDance employees, Zhang stated that he preferred "solitary activities like reading and daydreaming about what may be possible."

Chapter 33

Massage Therapist

The Story of Twitter and Square's Founders

"No matter what, expect the unexpected, and whenever possible, be the unexpected."
—*Lynda Barry*

Twitter is a social network and real-time communication platform launched in 2006 by Jack Dorsey. Today, millions use Twitter via the web and mobile devices to exchange bite-size updates of information called 'tweets,' which can also contain photos, videos, article links, and more. Twitter users follow other users they are interested in and see their updates on their home page. Jack Dorsey also co-founded Square in 2009 with his friend Jim McKelvey. Square is easy-to-use technology for mobile payment processing and credit card reading, and today, it is used by millions of small businesses to accept credit card payments, track sales and inventory, and receive other financial services.

Jack Dorsey was born and raised in St. Louis, Missouri. When he was a kid, he was fascinated with the world and wanted to learn everything about it. His parents got him a book called "Dove," which was about Robin Graham, a 16-year-old who sailed around the world on a boat by himself. He thought that was amazing and wanted to do the same thing, but there was no ocean in St. Louis.

Growing up, Jack loved the urban atmosphere that surrounded him. His love for St. Louis and its history led him to become obsessed with maps. He bought every map that he could find, hung them all over the walls in his room, and looked at them. He gathered tons of maps of St. Louis and his other favorite city, New York City, to which he had never been. He often wondered what was happening at a particular intersection or area or how to get down a road most efficiently. Jack's parents had a CB radio and a police scanner. Ambulances, fire trucks, and police cars constantly reported their location and what they were doing on the police scanner. Jack would take the information from the police scanner and plot it out on his paper maps, so he could watch where the police cars were going. But gradually, computers replaced paper maps, and Jack's parents got their first computer in 1985, so Jack taught himself just enough programming to build electronic maps, put dots on those maps, and make them move. After creating maps of police cars and ambulances riding around St. Louis, little by little, Jack found public databases on the internet that he could program into his maps. As he continued doing that, he learned how to automate more of it until he finally had a picture made of real-time data of a real city operating before him. Jack didn't know until he was about 17 that what he was doing was called dispatch, and the software he had created was dispatch software.

Along with his fascination with cities, Jack was interested in leaders of cities and mayors. So when he was about to go to college, he was torn between political science and computer science. Jack wanted to work for the government but was not quite sure if he would have any impact within a reasonable time. In contrast, Jack knew he could see the effect instantly by writing simulator software, so he decided to go with computer science.

In college, Jack was still fascinated by city visualization and passionate about building dispatch systems. After a lot of research, he eventually found the largest dispatch firm in the world called DMS. The company was in New York City and had a simple website with just their logo and name. Jack could not figure out how to contact them, but he really wanted to see what they were doing or potentially work for them. Influenced by the underground hacking culture of St. Louis, Jack hacked the DMS website and figured out a hole in it through which he found their corporate email list, including the email addresses of their CEO and chairman. He sent them emails and said, "Hey, I'm Jack Dorsey. You have a hole in your website. This is how to fix it. By the way, I write dispatch software if you're looking to hire!" A week later, the company invited Jack to New York City and offered him a job there. For Jack, it was like living his dream: working at the biggest dispatch firm in the world and writing software to visualize New York City. Jack started his job and transferred to New York University. After some time, however, he realized that he was learning a lot more and was moving faster outside the university than inside, so he decided to drop out.

After a while, Jack realized that he had a beautiful picture of the city, but there were no people in it. He wanted to see and feel the city on a personal level and know what its population was doing in real-time. To make that happen, he started making a simple prototype inspired by a service called live Journal, a simple blogging application that allowed people to compose a blog post, and then that post would go to a friend's page. Jack wanted to build an email pager similar to that application that would allow him to share what he was doing and see what his friends were up to. In 2000, Jack wrote some simple software to receive an email from his Blackberry and then send it out to an email list. He was very excited to test his software, but it turned out that not many had a BlackBerry, and no one really cared what he was up to. Jack felt he was the only one who wanted to share and receive information and decided to put this idea on the shelf and move on.

The dispatch company that Jack worked for moved to San Francisco, and Jack moved with it to the Bay Area and started living in Berkeley. Shortly after, his company began to fail because it had hired too many salespeople and only had five engineers. Most of those engineers were in Montreal, and Jack had to travel to Montreal to manage them. After his company folded in 2000, Jack did a lot of contract jobs in San Francisco, from coding for medical devices to the ticketing system of Alcatraz tours.

As Jack was writing codes for his contract jobs, his wrist started hurting, eventually becoming very painful. He was fearful that he was developing a carpal tunnel and started asking his friends what he should do. They suggested he should get a massage. However, instead of just getting massages, Jack decided to learn how to give massages and moved back to St. Louis to become a massage therapist! He enrolled in the Healing Arts Center in St. Louis and took 1000 hours of massage therapy classes until he became a licensed therapist.

Jack had planned to dedicate his life to massage therapy. But because he was still fed up with technology, he got a strange idea: do chair massages for software programmers, and while he was massaging their shoulders and wrists, he would also give them advice on their code; that way, he would be a massage and code therapist! Jack moved back to San Francisco in 2005 only to realize that not only was his idea stupid, but there were so many massage therapists there that he could not compete. So he went back to programming again.

Jack joined a company for three months, but much of what he was doing was on the backend, and he really didn't like the work. He had always wanted to do something with more direct interaction that his mom could see immediately. Jack kept working on random contract jobs until he discovered Odeo, a startup working on consumer podcasting. Jack had no interest in podcasting whatsoever, but he really liked the people running the company, especially its founder, Ev Williams, who had founded Blogger and sold it to Google a few years prior.

As soon as Jack started working at Odeo, he realized that no one else was passionate about the podcasting product they were developing either. Their business was not doing well, which created a situation for other ideas to bubble up as the whole team often went out and thought about what they really wanted to work on. They started having "hack days" to try to implement some of those ideas. The first thing that came to Jack's mind was his idea from back in 2000. He brought up his idea and said, "What if people could use something like SMS on the web to send what they're doing out in real-time to all the people interested in hearing about it?" Two of his colleagues agreed it was a good idea, and they presented it to the company. Odeo finally got behind Jack's idea, and he was given two weeks and one other programmer to write the software. Jack built a prototype and wrote the first tweet at the end of that two weeks, which invited his coworkers to follow him. The whole Odeo team came on and loved it. Little by little, Jack took coworkers from Odeo and brought them on the Twitter project until they spun it out as a separate company.

Jack and his colleagues used Twitter and then invited their friends who used it, and they then invited their own friends; Twitter's popularity kept boiling and boiling. In 2007, at the South by Southwest conference in Austin, Texas, all the influential bloggers and other people presenting used Twitter. In their sessions, they said, "The only way you will find out what sessions I'm attending and what bars I'm going to later in the evening is to follow me on this app called Twitter." That was the first South by Southwest that the press, including the New York Times and Wall Street Journal, attended, so many of their journalists started getting on Twitter. They later talked about Twitter, generating free publicity. The following year, the US presidential election was happening in 2008, and the campaigns got on Twitter too. By then, celebrities also started using the app to spread their messages directly to people.

In 2008, as the financial markets were crashing, Jack stepped down from the Twitter CEO role and became the company's chairman. Around the same time, he reconnected with Jim McKelvey, his first boss when he was 15 years old. Jim was doing glass arts back then but was very interested in tech. Jim said he wanted to build an electric car company, to which Jack said he had no idea how to do that, but it was an interesting idea, and they really wanted to work together on something. Sometime later, Jim called Jack and told him about his frustration. He had just lost a sale of a two-thousand-dollar piece of glass art because the woman who wanted to buy it could only pay with a credit card, and Jim couldn't accept credit cards. They both started wondering why he couldn't accept credit cards but soon realized that the payment industry was highly complicated. Still, building something that would allow Jim to accept a credit card seemed like an exciting challenge. So they set aside a month to work on that idea despite knowing nothing about the credit card industry and both being in debt.

They started searching on Google for how reading the cards worked. They figured that the magnetic strip on most credit cards was the same technology used in cassette tapes to play music. The strip was an audio track that software could decode into numbers that contained the credit card numbers and their expiration date. Then that number would be sent up to credit companies, like Visa, to check if funds were available, and if there were funds, they would be captured and sent to a bank account. After learning how reading credit cards worked, Jack and Jim realized that it wasn't that hard to build technology to enable everyone to accept credit cards. All mobile phones used to have a headphone jack on them back then, so in a month, they built a very early prototype of what is now known as a Square, a small credit card reader plugged into any device's audio jack. That simple thing worked.

But after making that prototype, they started reading about regulations and realized that they were against the industry standards by giving Square away for free without any sort of merchant account or monthly fees. They decided to push through anyway. All the financial institutions told them, "People are used to paying for these things. You're being foolish by leaving money on the table." But Jack and Jim stayed determined to enable everyone to accept credit cards.

Along the way, Jack realized that they were not building just a credit card terminal but actually a full point-of-sale system. The opportunity involved all the data that existed around a business and the potential insights driven by it, which could help business owners make better decisions. So, they spent the next few years developing a system to capture this data and give it to all the sellers.

When Square first launched, it had high adoption rates because it allowed businesses of all sizes to accept card payments anywhere instead of relying on cash and provided the most comprehensive free point-of-sale system. Over time, Square introduced new products, including Cash App (initially known as Square Cash), allowing users to send and receive money for free through a mobile application. Cash app recently also added support for Bitcoin and stock trading, while Square acquired several other companies, including the music streaming service Tidal and Afterpay, the Australian startup offering a "buy now, pay later" service.

While Jack was still Square's CEO, he also became Twitter's CEO again in 2015 and led the company in that role until he resigned in November 2021. During his time as CEO, Twitter reached hundreds of millions of active monthly users. Shortly after Jack resigned in late 2021, his other company, Square, changed its name to Block, Inc to represent "the neighborhood blocks where Square's sellers are, a blockchain, block parties full of music, obstacles to overcome, a section of code, building blocks, and tungsten cubes!"

Jack Dorsey is the only person to have co-founded and concurrently served as the CEO of two publicly-traded companies with valuations exceeding tens of billions of dollars. Jack has used his wealth for philanthropic causes, including donating $1 billion, or just under a third of his total wealth at the time, to relief programs related to the coronavirus pandemic in spring 2020. Jack always wanted to directly affect his parents' lives with the products he worked on and finally succeeded in achieving his goal; his mom has now tweeted him and said, "Hey Jack, I just used Square to pay at this coffee shop."

Chapter 34

The Jam Pad

The Story of Uber's Founders

"I'm Winston Wolfe. I solve problems."
—Mr. Wolf (Pulp Fiction, 1994 film)

Uber is an on-demand car and food delivery service. Users push a button on an iPhone or Android, and in a few minutes, a car appears. While today many people have tried Uber and are familiar with ride-sharing services, Uber was a groundbreaking idea in 2009 when it was started by Travis Kalanick and Garret Camp in San Francisco.

When Travis Kalanick was 18, he started tutoring for the SATs. The scores of the first person he assisted went up 400 points. After that, he started tutoring the whole neighborhood until one of his student's fathers invited him to start an SAT prep company with him. Their company was called "New Way Academy," and Travis created the course and did all the teaching while his business partner was in charge of the marketing. Travis would teach students who were only one year younger than him for eight hours on Saturdays. It wasn't just about the course material; he wanted to make his teaching engaging, inspiring, and funny. Travis even hired some teachers and trained them. It was a lot of fun until he got tired of filling in ABCD and decided to go to UCLA to study computer science.

At UCLA, Travis joined the computer science undergraduate association in late 1997. Its members used email to share files of music, video, and images with each other, but they thought it would be cool if there was a place to search for those things and got the idea to create the first peer-to-peer pirate software. So Travis and his peers built a multimedia search engine called Scour. Scour would crawl people's shared Windows directories and index the files. Then someone could search for Britney Spears, for example, and get the results. After clicking on a link, Scour pulled the files from other shared windows. It was the first peer-to-peer software and one of the most advanced pieces of technology on the internet.

In the beginning, Scour was only used by college students, but then it got a tremendous amount of usage from across the web. So, in 1998, Travis and some of his friends dropped out of UCLA to work full-time on Scour. But just when Scour was rapidly becoming more popular in 2001, it was sued for two hundred and fifty billion dollars by thirty-three of the largest media companies in the world. They knew that the lawsuit was a big liability and decided to resolve that litigation as soon as possible. They turned their technology off, declared Chapter 11 bankruptcy, and sold their company for about ten million dollars in a courtroom. Their bankruptcy court was like an auction; their company was sold in twenty minutes.

After Scour got sued and went out of existence, Travis decided to use his expertise in peer-to-peer technology to start a new company called Red Swoosh. Travis removed the interface from Scour, leaving the peer-to-peer backend technology there, which worked as a network stack that could move data more efficiently. Red Swoosh software took advantage of that increased bandwidth efficiency to enable users to transfer large media files, including music and videos. Because of that capability, Travis thought he could turn those thirty-three litigants who had sued them into customers that could use Red Swoosh to click on links to pull files while saving money on bandwidth. But it appeared Red Swoosh was a few years too early to market, and there were not many interested customers for it out there.

Travis started as an engineer, but he had to run everything himself when everyone else left the company. Since his company was all about enterprise software, he had to learn how to make enterprise sales even though he only had an engineering background. Travis couldn't pay himself for the first four years, so he had to live with his mom. Even with all his money-saving tricks, Red Swoosh was about to completely run out of money. Fortunately, when Scour was sued, a few billionaires were on its board, including Mark Cuban, the famous investor on the TV show Shark Tank. Travis reached out to Mark Cuban to save his company, and Mark invested one million dollars in Red Swoosh. The hard times eventually paid off, and in 2007, Travis sold Red Swoosh to another company for about $20 million.

After selling his company, Travis didn't want to be fully involved in running a new company again, but he was still interested in ideas, so he started angel investing for a year and a half. The entrepreneurs who pitched him or whom he'd invested in began creating a community at his house in San Francisco, which became like an open house; people would come by at any time of the day or night, even at 3:00 am to have jam sessions. They nicknamed his house the "Jam Pad," and it became a welcoming environment for entrepreneurs to come together and discuss problems they wanted to solve and the technology they wanted to create. Some people came when they needed to raise money or make their first sale.

Travis had an insanely curious personality, advised several startups in different areas, from labor on-demand to healthcare IT, and invested all of his money in ten of them. But when people asked him what was going on, he could only tell them about those ten startups and the people running them. That didn't feel authentic to him, which pushed him towards getting more involved with those companies. Around the same time, he watched a movie called "Vicky Cristina Barcelona" in the theater and found it brilliant. He walked out of the theater, searched for who had made that movie, and learned it was Woody Allen. He thought, "Woody Allen is older, but he still has his art and still has the energy to create. He still has brilliant ideas, and he's still sharing them with the world." Inspired by that, Travis decided to try again and do something big.

As Travis was looking for his next big thing, he started talking about ideas with his friend Garrett Camp. Garrett Camp had co-founded a company acquired by eBay, and was also looking for his next project. Travis and Garrett went to Paris in 2009 for a conference. While in Paris, they spent several days with their friends, riffing on ideas late into the night. One of those nights, Garret and Travis couldn't get a taxi and had to walk back to their hotel. Garret said, "I just want to push a button and get a ride." This got them talking about how it was similarly hard to get a taxi in San Francisco. Garret said, "Why don't we just buy a few limos, hire a few drivers, and make a little iPhone app where someone can just push a button, and a car appears in five minutes?" Travis said, "That sounds like an amazing idea!"

Travis and Garret went back to San Francisco and co-founded UberCab with $250 thousand of Garret's own money. In the beginning, Travis and Garret thought their business should be an on-demand cab service. While trying to hire private drivers, they realized that sharing the cost of a driver could make it more affordable, so their idea morphed into ride-hailing. They started UberCab very simply: they had a couple of cars cruise around San Francisco and told their friends whenever they needed, they could get a car by using their app on their mobile phones. It was as simple as pushing a button. Their friends who tried the service really liked it, and it quickly became apparent that UberCab could take off if it wasn't a limo company but a technology company for ride-sharing.

Travis's first role at UberCab was chief strategy officer, and, about a year later, he became the company's CEO. On the same day that Travis became CEO, UberCab received a Cease-and-Desist letter from the city of San Francisco and the state of California. There were many complaints from San Francisco taxicab operators, and the regulators were trying to shut them down. The taxi industry was very concerned about how UberCab could disrupt their business. But UberCab claimed it was not using yellow cabs, and in 2011, the company changed its name to Uber.

After starting out in San Francisco, Uber spread to other cities. Despite its simple start, scaling Uber was very complicated. In 2012, the company introduced UberX, a cheaper option that allowed people to use non-luxury vehicles, including their personal vehicles. By early 2013, Uber was available in thirty-five cities and continued to spread. Their services expanded from ride-hailing to food delivery (Uber Eats), package delivery, and freight transportation. As of the beginning of 2022, Uber is the largest ride-hailing company globally, with operations in over 900 metropolitan areas worldwide.

Travis resigned as CEO of Uber in the summer of 2017. Despite his resignation, he retained his seat on Uber's board of directors. In May 2019, Uber became a public company via an initial public offering. Uber's IPO price made it the highest-valued tech IPO since Facebook and Alibaba, giving it an initial market cap of $75 billion. Following the IPO, however, Uber's shares dropped, resulting in one of the biggest IPO first-day dollar losses. In December 2019, Travis resigned from Uber's board, and in the weeks leading up to his resignation, he reportedly sold off more than $2.5 billion of Uber stock, which was the majority of his shares.

In 2018, Travis started a venture fund called 10100. Shortly after initiating his venture fund, Travis announced that he had invested $150 million in City Storage Systems, which focused on redeveloping distressed real estate assets. He took the role of its CEO after the investment, and in the same year, City Storage Systems acquired a startup that worked on a "ghost kitchen" business. Ghost kitchens, also known as "virtual restaurants," are purpose-built facilities leased to restaurants and individuals to prepare food for delivery-only service. City Storage Systems ghost kitchen business operates under the name CloudKitchens. Travis has invested millions of dollars of his own money in CloudKitchens. After working for many years on media file sharing and ride sharing, Travis Kalanick wants to once again disrupt another industry, this time by sharing kitchens!

Chapter 35

Tip Bucket

The Story of Venmo's Founders

"It took me four years to paint like Raphael, but a lifetime to paint like a child."
—*Pablo Picasso*

Venmo is an app that many people use to pay their friends back by sending and accepting payments to or from others online. With Venmo, there is no wallet or fees, and users can connect a debit or credit card to the app and spend away. Venmo was created by two friends, Iqram Magdon-Ismail and Andrew Kortina, in 2009.

Iqram was born and raised in Africa and spent the first few years of his life in Zimbabwe, Zambia, and Uganda until he emigrated to the United States with his mom when he was fourteen. When Iqram first moved to the US, he tried to fit into society. He was pretty much silent throughout the day and didn't have many friends. After school, he would go to the park, stand next to the basketball court, and watch people play. While watching them for hours, he thought, "I want to get in this game. If only someone would let me play." Then one day, a guy came up to him and said, "Hey man, do you want to play with us?" Iqram was nervous but immediately said yes. That was his first basketball game in America, but he was welcome in more games after that.

Iqram went to a high school in Virginia and eventually got into the University of Pennsylvania to study computer science and theater. There, Iqram met Andrew during their freshman year. Initially, they didn't say much to each other. But every now and then, Iqram played guitar in his little dorm room, and one day Andrew came up to Iqram and said, "Hey, I saw you play guitar. Could you show me how to play?" Iqram said, "Yes, but I saw you lifting weights. Do you think you can show me how to do that?" They got to know each other and became friends and roommates. During the four years of college, Iqram and Andrew worked on several projects together. They were seniors when Facebook was launched at Harvard. As soon as Facebook launched, Andrew and Iqram got together and said, "Maybe we should do our own version of Facebook for UPenn here?" But before they did, Facebook came to their university as well.

After graduating from college, Iqram and Andrew explored many ideas and worked on a few. The first thing they did was to go around in Philadelphia, knocking on the doors of every restaurant and saying, "Hey, we'll make your website if you give us free food." Surprisingly, they found out that most restaurant owners were unwilling to give free food to get a website. Eventually, they decided to go to the same restaurants and instead say, "We'll make you a website for $200." All of a sudden, all those restaurants were interested. They had about a hundred restaurants online by the time they finished. In addition to making money to pay their rent, they learned how to sell and present their ideas to people through the process.

After some time, Iqram and Andrew realized that making websites for restaurants would not scale into something that could fund their lives. So, they decided to join a startup that could help them grow into what they wanted to do eventually; running their own company. They had multiple criteria for the startup that they were looking for. They thought it had to be one in a very early stage, and that hadn't raised significant funding but had enough to pay

$60K a year. It also had to be a team with less than six people, so they would essentially be amongst the founders to build the company together. Lastly, it should have a strong team of good engineers and designers so they could learn from them.

Iqram and Andrew scoured Y Combinator's, the famous startup incubator, to find first-class companies that were potential fits for them. They found a startup that had just graduated from Y Combinator and was in New York City, so Iqram and Andrew went up to NYC to talk to them. The company consisted of two guys who hired Iqram and Andrew right away. They worked 24/7, coding from the minute they got to the office to 4:00 am. Then they went home, took a shower, slept for a few hours, and repeated the same thing every day. That company eventually made some popular games, and Iqram and Andrew spent about eight months there learning how to build something that could scale.

After that, Iqram and Andrew separated and started doing their own things for a while. Iqram got a job in Philadelphia while Andrew stayed in New York. They started messaging each other again in 2009 to talk about getting together and making something. They set three goals for their next project. First, they wanted to do something in a trendy space, which at the time was mobile. It was the early days of the iPhone, and everyone wanted to get one. Their next criteria were something that they could use with each other. The final thing they wanted was a remote schedule so they could work whenever they wanted.

Iqram and Andrew kept brainstorming until they came up with the idea of their next project at a concert. They were in the mezzanine level of the concert, looking down at their friends' band. Towards the end of the show, their friend got on the microphone and said, "Hey, we're going to pass around a tip bucket. Please throw some cash in there to support the band. We appreciate it." Iqram and Andrew wanted to support the band, but they were at the top on the balcony and too lazy to go down. They also had to pay for their ride back home but didn't have enough cash and didn't want to run to an ATM. They started talking about how they could simplify that process. One of their ideas was, "What if we could just send money to the band with our cellphones?" That was when the idea of Venmo popped into their heads.

The next day they made a little sketch. They started with musicians and thought, "People can use their phones to text a short code, and bands could have a username that is synced with that code. In this way, bands could interact with their fans and sell their songs or get support." They wanted to take advantage of the trend that many people relied on their mobile phones. At the time, they both had blackberries, which were very popular even before the iPhone came out.

They sketched up their new idea, put a little pitch together, and then sat on it for a few weeks until they met again. About a month later, Iqram visited Andrew in New York City but left his wallet behind in Philadelphia as he was rushing to catch a bus to NYC. They were going to hang out and talk more about what they wanted to work on and have some fun. Iqram and Andrew spent that weekend going out, drinking, and dancing, but Andrew paid for the entire weekend. It was about $250, which was a lot of money for them since they both were living paycheck to paycheck and had part-time jobs, and Andrew needed that money back quickly. Sitting at a bar before Iqram caught his bus back to Philadelphia on that Sunday night, they both thought, "Why can't we send each other's money through our BlackBerrys?" They then realized that it was something they could use with each other, and that idea got them really excited. Instead of sketching further or putting slide decks together, they decided to build it. From that day forward, aside from their part-time jobs, they spent every waking hour working on a prototype that would allow them to send money to each other.

Iqram and Andrew designed the first version of Venmo so people could send money by phone numbers. It worked entirely over SMS; sending money to someone was just like sending them a text message. All they needed was a phone number, an amount, and a note. As soon as someone got money attached to their phone number, it would be on hold until they created an account. They launched the first version of Venmo in August 2009. Once they had the prototype, they faced a new challenge: how to get people to trust them with their financial information when using Venmo. They went to restaurants and put their credit card down, then the waiter would bring the cheque to someone's table and say, "This meal was on that guy," and point at Iqram and Andrew. Iqram would then go over to the table and say, "Hey, this one was on me. Can I have five minutes of your time to talk about this new thing I'm working on? It's an app called Venmo, which is a way to pay each other when we're at a restaurant. Here is how it works. If you're ever in this situation, you can use it with each other." He didn't force people to pay him back. Two out of every five times, people would actually get their phones and say, "That's kind of cool!" and would pay him back. Later, Iqram would send a little marketing email saying, "Next time you're out, please use Venmo again." Iqram and Andrew got the first five hundred Venmo users by doing this. Slowly, they started to see that one of these people from the restaurants would send money to someone they didn't know every now and then. They realized that their idea was working, and all Venmo needed was a good marketing team.

Iqram and Andrew needed money to hire people, but they couldn't get any investments when they first started out. So they tried to find more use cases for their app. They seriously thought about food trucks for a month because they accepted only cash, so they ran around to all the food trucks and tried to convince them to sign up for Venmo and use it. When they were pitching to investors in a meeting, someone asked, "So what's your market?" Iqram said, "Every food truck in the world!" After gaining no traction with food trucks, Iqram and Andrew explored charities. They thought charities could use Venmo to collect money for their foundations, but that didn't help either.

As Iqram and Andrew struggled to raise money, one of their advisors helped them conceptualize the notion of trust by creating a new feature. The new feature let people create a group of their friends on Venmo and share money with them. With this new feature, they garnered excitement from investors and quickly raised two hundred thousand dollars. After raising money, Iqram and Andrew started working on Venmo full-time and hired their first employee. They launched the new Venmo app in 2012, which was no longer an SMS only. Now, it was fast and had a social nature. Friends could watch the logs and see their friends using Venmo with each other and leaving casual, friendly notes. Venmo removed all transaction costs, allowing people to send money online for free. This made it a major hit for people that didn't carry cash, like students and teens. Venmo started growing virally without them having to run around telling everybody about the app.

As their transaction volume grew, their costs were growing exponentially too. They were spending lots of their invertors' money to keep running transactions for free. They had some plans for making revenue, but they couldn't figure out a promising way to become profitable. Venmo was close to being shut down, so Iqram and Andrew suddenly decided to explore acquisition. Just in time, another online payment provider company named Braintree showed interest in buying Venmo. A few months after Venmo officially launched, Braintree acquired it for $26 million, and eight months later, PayPal acquired Braintree for $800 million.

Today Venom is still part of PayPal. Despite the increasing competition over the years, Venmo has remained the most popular money transfer app among people under thirty-five. As of 2022, Venmo has millions of users and processes billions of dollars in total payment volume annually. Since the PayPal deal, Iqram and Andrew have moved on to other ventures. Iqram co-founded Ense, an audio-based social media platform, and Andrew co-founded Fin.com, a work insights platform that provides enterprise data insights for operations teams.

Chapter 36

No Games, No Gimmicks!

The Story of WhatsApp's Founders

"The successful warrior is the average man with laser-like focus."
—*Bruce Lee*

WhatsApp is a free messaging app that uses data to let users text, chat, and share media, including voice messages and video, with individuals or groups. Now the most popular messaging app in many countries worldwide, WhatsApp was started by two former Yahoo employees, Jan Koum and Brian Acton, in 2009.

Jan was born and raised in a small village outside of Kiev, Ukraine, in 1976. In 1992, when he turned 16, he and his mother immigrated to the United States due to the anti-Semitic environment. They settled in Mountain View, California, and got a small two-bedroom apartment with government assistance. Since Jan's dad never made it over to America, his mom got a babysitting job, and Jan swept the grocery store floor to help make ends meet. When Jan's mother was diagnosed with cancer, they lived off her disability allowance.

In high school, Jan taught himself about computers by purchasing manuals from a used book store and returning them when he was done. At 18, he enrolled at San Jose State University and started working for Ernst and Young as a security tester. He met early Yahoo employee Brian Acton in 1997 when he was on an assignment for Ernst and Young. Six months later, Brian helped him get a job as an infrastructure engineer at Yahoo. Jan was still at San Jose State University when, two weeks into his job at Yahoo, one of the company's servers broke. His manager called him and asked him to help, but Jan answered, "I'm in class." His manager said, "What are you doing in class? Come into the office right now." After that, he dropped out of school and started working at Yahoo full-time.

At Yahoo, Jan sat at a desk across from Brian. They liked each other's styles and became fast friends. When Jan's mother died of cancer in 2000, Brian reached out and offered support. Jan remained at Yahoo for nine years, rising to become manager of infrastructure engineering and learning how to scale up a server and what makes a good or bad product. During their time at Yahoo, Jan and Brian watched the company go through multiple ups and downs. They saw how Yahoo became a successful company and then later declined.

Coincidently, Jan and Brian both left Yahoo around the same time in 2007 and took some time off. Brian moved to New York with his girlfriend for a year while Jan was dawdling and eating into his savings from Yahoo. During that time, Jan fell in love with his Nokia phone, which he jailbroke and installed admin software on. This showed all the advanced things someone could do with the phone that they couldn't do straight out of the box.

Jan started traveling the world at the end of 2008, visiting Russia, Argentina, Ukraine, Hungary, and other countries. He was gone for three months on and off. But he found staying in touch with his friends during his travels was very hard, especially in Argentina. The country code in Argentina was particularly complicated to dial, and he wished he had a better way to stay connected with his friends.

Jan's birthday was coming up in February 2009, so he got himself an iPhone as an early birthday present. The first iPhone had been released just a few months before. Since Jan was bored and had a lot of free time, he started tinkering with his iPhone. He wanted to figure out what he could do with it, so he installed a coding program on his Mac and built some simple apps. He then realized that iPhone was basically a tiny computer with full internet connectivity that had a lot of potential and decided to make an app for it.

Back then, the first message in a conversation on popular messengers like Yahoo or AOL was usually, "Hey, are you there?" Yahoo messenger had a feature that showed a message if the person was away from the keyboard or busy or in a meeting. Jan wanted to take that concept of status and apply it to mobile phones so people could check a person's status before starting a phone call or sending a message. The status could show things like if a person was traveling, their battery was low, or they were at the gym, and so on. Jan chose the name WhatsApp for his app because it sounded like "what's up" and incorporated WhatsApp on his birthday, February 24th.

Jan could do the backend himself, but he needed an iPhone developer. A friend introduced him to a developer in Russia, and together they built an app that would hook into the address book and show a status next to individual names. The first version of WhatsApp failed horribly. People downloaded it, mostly because there were no other similar apps back then, but nobody used it. Jan added different features like setting status to automatically change at a certain time, but none worked. Then in the summer of 2009, Apple introduced push notifications, allowing users to be pinged when they were not using an app. Before that, if a person wanted the application to wake up, they had to tap on the icon. Jan changed WhatsApp so that everyone in the user's network would be notified when a user's status changed, and noticed that after the change, people were using the status as a way to communicate with each other. They would change the status to things like "I'm going to a bar," and then the status change would broadcast to all other people in their address book who used WhatsApp. Jan thought that was interesting and decided he should build a messaging app to facilitate communication.

After WhatsApp became a messaging app, Brian joined the team. He put his own savings in the company and persuaded five former friends at Yahoo to invest $250,000 in seed funding. Jan made Brian a co-founder and gave him a stake. They launched the messaging version of WhatsApp at the end of the summer of 2009, but WhatsApp didn't have many features in the beginning. There were no group messages, sending media, or recording voice messages; only text messaging. Jan and Brian used a trick to get their first users. The Apple store had a category for new apps, and back then, making small changes to the name would trigger an app as new. Every few days, they submitted a new app version, so they always showed up on top of the new apps category.

WhatsApp quickly took off and gained a large user base. SMS services, especially international SMS, were expensive in those days. People could use Skype to send messages, but Skype only worked on a desktop. There was no other practical way for people in different countries to communicate in real-time. Another problem with SMS was that people could only send 160 characters at a time, and it did not work well across different platforms. On the other hand, the WhatsApp messaging service was free and super reliable, with visual indicators to show the message was successfully delivered to the device it was sent to.

Jan and Brian had left Yahoo with enough savings to live off for a long time, but they had to avoid losing too much money since WhatsApp was free and generated no profits. To save $20 a month, Jan had asked one of his friends to let them use his server when they started WhatsApp because saving $20 a month was a big deal for him. But as WhatsApp messaging was growing quickly, his friend told Jan that they needed to get their own server. Jan was reluctant to pay for his own server but finally had to.

Jan and Brian decided to hire additional staff when they realized their app had become popular. Most of the people they convinced to join them were unemployed or were not doing well at the time. One of Jan's friends was involved with another startup that wasn't going anywhere. He was in LA, but his in-laws were in the Bay Area, so the combination of his wife wanting to move closer to her parents and him needing a full-time job made him decide to accept Jan's offer. Jan hired another guy who complained how he hated his job and how his employer was screwing him over by promising him stock options and never delivering. Jan and Brian kept hiring people referred by their friends; none of them were doing much when they joined WhatsApp. They were a small band of outcasts who got together to build a great product.

WhatsApp started out with iPhone, but as an immigrant who recently traveled to many countries, Jan knew that other smartphones were out there. Back then, Nokia and Blackberry were the major smartphone platforms everywhere except North America, and Android barely existed. They had to find people who could build for those platforms, but nobody in Silicon Valley even heard of Nokia. So, they found people in Europe and developed WhatsApp for Nokia and Android by the end of the summer of 2010. After building multiple platforms, they started adding features, focusing on creating what people wanted, like group chat, multimedia, and voice messages. There was no cheap and reliable way to send pictures and videos over the phone back then. Enabling that helped WhatsApp to take off. WhatsApp quickly started growing organically without any marketing or press coverage. It became especially popular in lesser developed countries that heavily relied on SMS texting. Since people were using WhatsApp organically without any marketing, Jan and Brian could spend their time with their heads down building their app while ignoring the press and the spotlight.

Jan and Brian deeply cared about user privacy from the beginning. They didn't want to collect their users' personal data because they were not advertisement-driven. Influenced by their experience at Yahoo, Jan and Brian both believed advertising was awful and chose to avoid it. Brian once wrote a note on a piece of paper that read "no ads, no games, no gimmicks," and Jan kept that note taped to his desk. They were committed to building a simple and useful product with a great consumer experience.

Because of Jan and Brian's experience running the company efficiently, they could cover the cost of electricity, internet bandwidth, and servers. But their expenses started going up when they had to hire people. Saving money tricks didn't work anymore, and Jan and Brain knew they needed some money. Rather than targeting users with ads, they decided to charge a dollar for downloading WhatsApp for iPhones while keeping everything else free. That small payment for app downloads enabled them to pay their bills. Around 2011, venture capitalists began knocking on WhatsApp's door and asking to invest. But Jan rejected them and said they didn't really need the money, making those venture capitalists want to invest even more. Eventually, Brian and Jan decided that they had better accept some money so they had it in their bank account if they really needed it. They got the funding from Sequoia Capital, one of the most prominent venture capital firms in Silicon Valley.

The rapid growth of WhatsApp continued, and by the end of 2013, the app reached 400 million active monthly users. In February 2014, just five years after Jan incorporated WhatsApp, Facebook announced they would acquire WhatsApp for $19 billion, the largest acquisition of a venture-backed company in history. WhatsApp had only about 50 employees when the announcement came, and Jan, who owned almost 45% of the company, was suddenly worth about $7 billion. Facebook assured Jan and Brian that WhatsApp would remain ad-free. Still, after the acquisition, Jan joined Facebook's board and continued to champion the rights of WhatsApp users.

Over time, WhatsApp added voice and video calls and stopped charging users a $1 annual subscription fee. By the middle of 2014, WhatsApp had become the most popular messaging app globally, a title it has kept as of 2022. Brian left Facebook in 2017 to start a nonprofit group named the Signal Foundation, which developed the WhatsApp competitor Signal, while Jan announced he would be leaving Facebook a year later in 2018 and stepped down from the WhatsApp CEO position.

Chapter 37

Campus Trailer

The Story of Yahoo's Founders

"Sit loosely in the saddle of life."
—*Robert Louis Stevenson*

Yahoo was one of the pioneers of the early internet era in the 1990s and is famous for its web portal and email services. As one of the oldest names on the internet, it has consistently been one of the most popular websites. The company was founded in 1995 by two Stanford graduate students, Jerry Yang and David Filo.

Jerry was born in Taiwan and spent his early childhood there. Jerry's father died when he was two, and his mother decided to start over in the US. She moved from Taiwan to San Jose, California, as a single parent with two young boys and a few suitcases. Jerry was ten years old at the time, and the only English word he knew was "shoe." Jerry got his first computer when he was in high school, and he and his brother figured out how to program on it, but he didn't get deeper into computers until college.

Jerry went to Stanford University to study electrical engineering. At Stanford, Jerry met David Filo in 1990 when both were graduate students. They connected over a project David managed to complete almost overnight, leading Jerry to notice that David was pretty bright. They soon became very close friends. After getting their master's in electrical engineering, both Jerry and David decided to stay at Stanford for their PhDs, focusing on computer design.

During their second year, their adviser taught at the Stanford campus in Kyoto, Japan, for three months, and he took Jerry and David with him. When Jerry and David returned to Stanford in the fall of 1992, they set up a tiny office in a university trailer with two desks, two computer stations, and two sets of golf clubs. They also had one sleeping bag, which they used for rotating naps. In their on-campus trailer at Stanford, David and Jerry were supposed to spend time researching algorithms for faster and more efficient digital chip design for their PhD thesis. But they procrastinated while their adviser was on sabbatical.

The internet had been around since 1973, but it remained obscure until the 1990s. Mosaic, the first graphical interface tailored to the web, was created in 1993. When Jerry and David found Mosaic, they started playing on the internet like everyone else, and their PhD research wasn't so interesting after discovering the web. After some time, Jerry and David noticed that although there were plenty of exciting sites, there was no proper online organization system. Because of that, they could not find the sites they had previously visited if they wanted to view them again. So, they decided to develop something that kept track of what they surfed and created a list of websites. Jerry converted that list into HTML and put it on the web so other people could use their directory of websites. They called it "Jerry's Guide to the World Wide Web."

Jerry and David organized the web so that everyday computer users could understand it. Their list of websites was organized into topics. At the top, there were broad categories covering subjects like business, health, entertainment, education, and computers, and then there were subcategories in each of those categories. They also created a search engine by which people could find their desired website simply by typing in the right keywords. They spent more and more time in their trailer, finding and organizing sites on the still chaotic internet. In 1994, they started out with a couple hundred websites, but it grew to a few thousand and then a hundred thousand. They spent hours cataloging the web and looking at web links instead of working on their thesis. They even slept on the floor of their trailer, and since they shared a sleeping bag, one worked while the other was sleeping, and then they would switch.

Jerry and David made their website directory for their own use, just as a hobby. But within a couple of months, thousands of people from forty different countries were using their website directory every day; they even suggested more sites to be added to their list. As time went on, the web's growth accelerated, and so the number of people who used their directory multiplied too.

Jerry and David got tired of typing Jerry's Guide to the World Wide Web because it was so long, and soon, they realized they had chosen the wrong name for their project. David said, "Let's find a shorter name." They locked themselves in the trailer with a dictionary and decided to find a name that started with Y and A, which stood for "yet another." They landed on Yahoo, which meant somebody who's very rude and uncivilized. Jerry and David thought they were a couple of Yahoos working on the web when they were supposed to work on their thesis, so they decided to go with that name.

Creating a company was the last thing on Jerry and David's minds. But their computers were running crazy as Yahoo started to explode, and they had to spend twenty-three hours a day in their trailer office to keep things going. They realized that they couldn't keep doing that for free. At the same time, Stanford University started making complaints about increased network traffic crashing their systems, and they asked Jerry and David to move off the campus.

Netscape, the company that owned Mosaic browser, had raised funding in 1994 and was the hottest story in Silicon Valley. Oher venture capitalists were looking for the next internet thing, without even knowing what the internet was. When Jerry and David started considering Yahoo as a business, not a hobby, they got a call from Sequoia Capital, one of Silicon Valley's most highly regarded venture capital firms. Sequoia Capital included successful companies like

Apple, Oracle, and Cisco among its investments. But for the first time, Sequoia Capital wanted to invest in a company that was giving away their product for free because they saw the internet as a new medium and wanted to be part of it.

In addition to venture capital firms, Jerry and David found several other companies more than ready to talk deals. AOL and Netscape were among the companies interested in buying Yahoo. Suddenly they had to decide; sell Yahoo and continue their PhDs, or keep working on Yahoo as a venture-backed startup. It was hard for Jerry to put his PhD on hold, but he knew they couldn't put Yahoo on hold; otherwise, they would never have such an opportunity again. The duo dropped out and decided to leave the Stanford campus and run Yahoo as a venture-backed startup. Jerry and David incorporated Yahoo! Inc in 1995. Sequoia Capital gave them a million dollars to start and took 25% of the company for that money. They moved out of their campus home and into a new office. Now with ever more web traffic, they needed staff. After putting together a core team of nine, Jerry and David hired a CEO and took the official title of "Chief Yahoo" for themselves.

Up to that point, the internet hadn't been commercialized much. Jerry and David wanted to let their users continue using Yahoo for free, but they knew that they had to find a way to make money to pay back their investors and expand their company. So they started thinking of advertising, but introducing advertising to the web was a controversial move back then. They decided to give it a shot, and if people stopped using it, they would know it was the wrong thing to do. There were some complaints when Yahoo started using advertisements, but it turned out it wasn't a big deal. They did partnerships with companies like Reuters and became the first worldwide online news feed. With more funds and employees, Yahoo took off very quickly. In April 1996, Yahoo went public with less than fifty employees. On the first day of IPO, Yahoo stock on the Nasdaq exchange opened at $13 and closed at $33 a share. From a humble start in a campus trailer, Yahoo became the most valued internet company in the world.

In 1997, Jerry visited China for the first time to speak at a conference. The Chinese government sent a ministry official to be his tour guide. That tour guide happened to be Jack Ma, who founded Alibaba several months later. Jack Ma took Jerry to the Great Wall of China and then to do karaoke. Jerry realized that Jack Ma was very interested in what was going on with the internet, and the two hit it off, discussing the growth of the web, but lost touch after that trip. From 2000 to 2003, Yahoo tried to build a business in China. But they realized that they were competing against powerful local competitors and felt it was easier to invest in a proven winner in China. Alibaba was one of the most successful Chinese internet companies at the time. Jerry found out that Alibaba was headed by his tour guide Jack Ma, so they reunited after about six years on a commercial battleground. In 2005, under Jerry's direction, Yahoo purchased a 40% stake in Alibaba for $1 billion. By that deal, Alibaba was valued at five billion dollars, which was the highest valuation for an internet company at the time. Years later, Yahoo made billions of dollars selling its stake in Alibaba.

Yahoo was one of the first companies to embrace banner ads, which was the first significant revenue stream coming directly from the internet. In the beginning, companies would rent space on the Yahoo homepage like a billboard. Yahoo started charging its advertisers based on impressions or how many times their banner ads were seen by users as the technology improved. That mechanism encouraged Yahoo to keep its users on its own website for as long as possible. In a way, banner ads came into conflict with the very first purpose of Yahoo, which was to help people find the best website for any given topic.

In 1996, two Stanford PhD students, Larry Page and Sergey Brin, developed an algorithm called PageRank that could determine the relative importance of a given web page based on how many other pages linked back to it. It was a very effective algorithm, but ironically it was too effective for Yahoo. When Larry Page and Sergey Brin tried to sell PageRank for just $1 million to Yahoo, they were surprised that Yahoo executives were not interested. They argued that using Page-

Rank would hurt Yahoo's business because people would find whatever they were looking for too fast, hence, seeing fewer banner ads in the process, which would reduce Yahoo's revenue. Larry Page and Sergey Brin decided to start their own company and developed their own search engine called Google. Over the next two years, Google refined its product and rapidly gained popularity due to its high quality. During the same time, Yahoo made millions of dollars from banner ads, but most of what it earned was spent on generating content for its portals. Yahoo neglected its directory and started licensing the Google search engine from 1998 onwards. Still, Yahoo was making so much money from the banner ads that it didn't mind paying Google for search functions.

In late 2000, Google came up with its targeted paid search system, AdWords. Suddenly Google became Yahoo's biggest competitor. Two years later, Yahoo offered to acquire Google for $3 billion. But Larry Page and Sergey Brin made a counteroffer of $5 billion, essentially proposing a merger between equal companies. Yahoo did not accept that counteroffer and moved on to make its own paid search engine. However, it took Yahoo a few years to do so, and by that time, it was way behind Google for ad revenue. What Yahoo could've acquired for $5 billion in 2003 is worth over one and a half trillion dollars in 2022.

The rise of Google led the board to appoint Jerry as interim CEO in 2007. While Yahoo was struggling to catch up to Google, Microsoft offered to buy Yahoo for $44 billion in 2008. Jerry had no desire to sell Yahoo, and the negotiations with Microsoft were difficult. Once those negotiations failed, Yahoo's stock price started plunging. Jerry resigned from both the CEO position and his position as "Chief Yahoo" in 2009 but remained on Yahoo's board of directors. In January 2012, Jerry left Yahoo, resigning from the board and all his other positions at the company. After leaving Yahoo, Jerry founded a venture capital company named AME Cloud Ventures, and in July 2021, was elected the chair of the Stanford University Board of Trustees.

Over the years, Yahoo pioneered several new internet services. But according to many, trying to be everything to everyone was Yahoo's downfall. After several years of struggle with the competition, Yahoo agreed to sell its core operating business to Verizon for $5 billion in cash in 2016. As of 2022, Yahoo is still among the most prominent internet brands and one of the most highly trafficked websites worldwide despite its mistakes and setbacks.

Chapter 38

Cry For Help

The Story of Yelp's Founders

"To succeed, jump as quickly at opportunities as you do at conclusions."
—*Benjamin Franklin*

Yelp is a social site for everything local, from lists of restaurants to hotels, dentists, and gyms. Founded in July of 2004 by former PayPal employees Jeremy Stoppelman and Russel Simmons, Yelp compiles word-of-mouth suggestions for local businesses and services, covering hundreds of different cities worldwide.

After graduating with a bachelor's degree in computer engineering from the University of Illinois at Urbana-Champaign, Jeremy Stoppelman joined the @Home Network, the first cable internet company. It was a big hit for a few months, but when he realized it would never be a huge success, he joined Elon Musk's small startup X.com in Silicon Valley. When Jeremy met Elon, he wondered how X.com, a little online bank, would take down Visa and MasterCard, but he was interested in working in that sector, so he stayed on. X.com eventually merged with another startup named Confinity, and together they became PayPal, and Jeremy became its

VP of engineering. PayPal was eventually sold to eBay in 2002 for $1.5 billion.

After eBay bought PayPal, Jeremy started thinking about his next step. There wasn't a lot of startup activity going on in 2002-2003 because of the dot-com bubble crash. So, Jeremy decided to go to business school. He applied to a few schools and got into Harvard, then after studying for his MBA for a year, Jeremy returned to the Bay Area for a summer internship. He was interested in an up-close look at the very beginning of a startup's life, which he didn't have exposure to at X.com and PayPal. He reconnected with Max Levchin, PayPal's co-founder and former CTO, and his former boss. Max Levchin had a small startup incubator, and Jeremy started an internship there. Within a couple of months, Max had Jeremy brainstorming and trying to develop new consumer internet ideas. That summer, Jeremy reconnected with Russ Simmons, the software engineer he knew from PayPal, and they started working together in the incubator. They played around with a bunch of ideas and noticed that Craigslist was killing the newspapers. At the same time, there was the context of consumer reviews with Amazon and the rise of social networks like Friendster and MySpace. They felt that Yellow Pages business was ripe for disruption in 2004 and thought, "What if we merge some of those consumer reviews with a social network?"

Jeremy and Russ started brainstorming to figure out a better alternative to the Yellow Pages and a way to get people to share consumer reviews about local businesses. They thought, "What if you could ask your friends for recommendations? Wouldn't that build a base of word-of-mouth knowledge? And allow you to find a local business? It'd be like the Yellow Pages but driven by consumer sentiment." The idea of connecting socially and adding a layer of consumer reviews seemed promising. The prospect excited them enough that they started building a website. Jeremy deferred his business school and committed to working with Russ. They were financed by Max Levchin's incubator and got $1 million to start.

Jeremy and Russ thought their service should be built around questions and answers. Someone would ask a question like, "Do you know a good doctor in San Francisco?" and their friends would respond. Russ, who was doing the coding, asked Jeremy, "Should we have a feature to allow people to write a review without being asked anything?" Jeremy was adamant that no one would ever write a review for fun. But he wanted to be open to his co-founder's idea, so he said, "Okay, include this feature somewhere in there." So, they buried the feature in their site as an extra way for users to write reviews without being asked a question.

They built the website in three months and were just a few weeks away from launching it when they began looking for a domain name. Jeremy was obsessed with Yocal, which sounded like local. But, despite trying hard, he couldn't get it. Someone suggested to Jeremey and Russ, "What do you think of Yelp?" Their initial reaction was, "We don't know. It sounds like a cry for help!" Initially, they thought Yelp had a negative connotation, but after thinking more about it, they realized it was short, easy to spell, and memorable. It also sounded like a combination of Yellow Pages and help, which their idea was all about, and was the only name they had, so ultimately, they went with Yelp.

Unfortunately, as soon as Yelp launched, Jeremy realized that people disliked the site. Most people thought it was a cool concept, but having a third-party website email out your friends and collect reviews just didn't make a lot of sense to them. People felt it was easier to just directly email their friends. Disappointed, Jeremy and Russ began to look at how people had used their new site. As Jeremy looked into their database, he realized that their little feature that allowed users to write reviews on their own was pretty popular. It appeared that some users became addicted to reviewing; they would write five to ten reviews in one sitting. He thought some people might enjoy writing reviews. Jeremy and Russ started to reshape Yelp into a platform for people to share their opinions online. It took them four months to complete the changes, and they launched the new version in February 2005. As soon as the website came up, people in San Francisco started reviewing places and discovering things in the city that they didn't know about.

Jeremy wanted to get direct feedback from their users and decided to meet with some of them and invited two Yelp users to a meetup. He expected that their early adopters would be tech guys but was surprised to find two social women passionate about finding new and cool things in San Francisco. They had a drink together and talked about their experience using Yelp. After that experience, Jeremy thought it would be good to get a hundred of these early users together for an event. They rented out a venue, brought together a hundred of their early users, and put together an event called the "Yelp Elite" launch party. Many of them brought a plus-one, and some of those people started using Yelp afterward. As Yelp became popular in San Francisco, they took advantage of more funding and expanded to other cities. They started throwing events across the United States and Canada, which helped Yelp grow community by community.

By 2009, Yelp became so popular that Google offered to buy it for $550 million. Yahoo countered that offer with a $1 billion check, and Yelp refused both. Instead, Yelp went public in 2012, with almost $1.5 billion market capitalization. After Google's failed attempt to buy Yelp, a brand-new application popped up on everybody's Android phone: Google Places app. It was very similar to Yelp, so, Yelp turned to the government and claimed that Google favored its own content in search results and was scraping data from Yelp for its own Google Places service, spurring antitrust investigations. After that, Google stopped competing against Yelp, and Yelp has flourished, growing its global user base, reaching over 200 million reviews as of 2022.

Chapter 39

Video Dating

The Story of YouTube's Founders

"It's not the size of the dog in the fight, it's the size of the fight in the dog."
—*Mark Twain*

YouTube is a free video-sharing website and the second largest search engine behind Google search. Anyone with access to a computer or mobile device and an internet connection can watch YouTube content and share their own. Today, it's owned by Google, but in 2004 it was a small startup co-founded by three former PayPal colleagues, Chad Hurley, Steve Chen, and Jawed Karim.

Chad Hurley started looking for a job after graduating from college with a graphic design degree in 1999. He read about a small company in Palo Alto, California, working on a payment solution for Palm Pilots. The company was looking for a graphic designer to design the interface for their new product, PayPal. Chad sent them his resume, and, a week later, he moved to California and joined a group of about ten people working at PayPal. Chad was the only designer, so he created all their designs, from the first interface for their website to credit cards and T-shirts.

At PayPal, Chad met Steve and Jawed, two of the first engineers. Both Steve and Jawed had studied computer science at the University of Illinois at Urbana–Champaign, the same school that some of PayPal's founders graduated from. Steve was born in Taiwan and came to the US when he was eight years old, and Jawed had a similar story. He was born in a Bangladeshi family and had immigrated to the US as a child. They all jumped into the world of startups, and PayPal was their first experience in Silicon Valley. Chad, Steve, and Jawed worked on several projects together there and got the chance to see how the company formed from the very beginning.

In 2002, PayPal went public and eventually was acquired by eBay for $1.5 billion. After the acquisition, Chad decided to take some time off, and he got married and settled down in Menlo Park. Steve stayed at PayPal for another two years until he joined Facebook, which was still an early-stage startup. He worked there for about three months, then began thinking about new opportunities. Steve had learned just about everything from PayPal and thought it was the time to start exploring and doing something new.

In late 2004, Chad, Steve, and Jawed reconnected and started talking about what they wanted to do next. They were all around the same age and looking to do something new. They started meeting up occasionally, trying to find out what opportunities were out there that would align with their interests. In the beginning, they had no idea what they wanted to build, so they kept getting together at Chad's house or having dinners in Palo Alto, spending a few hours just throwing out ideas.

At the time, people were sharing photos publicly on sites like Flickr, which was still relatively new. Chad, Steve, and Jawed thought the community built around images was fascinating, and there had to be a similar opportunity for video. Finally, they got an idea: making a video dating website where people could meet each other through video profiles. Instead of posting personal pictures, they thought people could post a video on their dating website to introduce themselves, and others would see and interact with them. They came up with the name YouTube for their website and bought the domain name on Valentine's Day, February 14th, 2005. "You" represented user-generated content, and "Tube" represented TV.

In about three months, they had built the initial version of YouTube and launched their video dating site in May 2005. However, they didn't get a single video uploaded in the first week. Nobody introduced themselves using YouTube because it turned out people didn't like to sit in front of a webcam and talk about who they were and what they were looking for. Hoping to get some videos posted, they put some flyers around the Stanford campus, but they only got a few crazy videos from the dorm. They were so desperate for some actual dating videos that they turned to Craigslist in Los Angeles and Las Vegas, encouraging people to upload videos of themselves in exchange for a $20 gift. Still, they didn't get a single reply.

After a week, it was clear that the video dating site wasn't going to work. However, Chad, Steve, and Jawed noticed that some users were uploading different kinds of videos, like their dogs or vacations, and using YouTube to share them. So, they quickly ripped everything out to convert YouTube from a dating video site into a general video sharing site. The back end of the site was still exactly the same. They just changed the search function; instead of searching by age or gender, now people could search for whatever they wanted. They also changed YouTube's look to how it exists today: a video player with a set of actions, comments, and related videos. They had completely revamped the website within a month, making it more open and general.

The new version of YouTube worked because, back then, video clips were scattered all over the internet, and there was no good way to share them as they were too big to email. Another big problem was that people first had to install the right video player to play a clip. The breakthrough with YouTube was that it streamlined video encoding into one format. YouTube videos were seamlessly played for the viewers, so they didn't have to worry about what type of video player they were using.

Chad, Steve, and Jawed started seeing traction. Their views and uploaded videos were doubling every week. However, every time somebody viewed a video on YouTube, they had to pay for it. Three people were building something with high requirements for the back end, from the storage in the data centers to the computational power, and they were trying to pay for all of that with their own credit cards. Coming off of PayPal, they could support themselves while they took some time to build the initial product. But things got more difficult when Jawed left YouTube to continue his education at Stanford.

Besides the high cost, YouTube was competing with other early online video players like Vimeo and Google Video. Chad and Steve decided to focus on short clips and speed so people could see a video and share it with others as quickly as possible. From PayPal, they had learned that people loved taking a payment button and putting it on their own websites or auctions, so they tried to do the same thing with YouTube, allowing their users to take their YouTube link and put it on their websites.

Back then, MySpace was still the most popular social networking platform. MySpace users started using YouTube once they found out they could embed videos onto their profiles. All they had to do was just copy and paste a small code into their profiles, and then, their video was seamlessly integrated. YouTube didn't charge for that but put its logo on their videos so others could see. After a while, so many MySpace users started using YouTube that YouTube was going viral on MySpace for free, so they didn't need money for marketing. YouTube was being used by more and more MySpace users, and videos became so popular that Myspace banned YouTube from being used on its platform in December 2005. Chad and Steve found a phone number and an email in the frequently asked questions of the MySpace customer support page. They put it on the front page of YouTube with this message: "Contact this number if you have any problems with your MySpace videos." MySpace received so many phone calls and emails that they turned around their decision just after two days and permitted YouTube to be used in their website again.

Chad and Steve had recruited many of their friends from PayPal and promised to pay them whenever they got funding. They all had a little bit in their bank accounts and could work for six months without demanding a salary. They still didn't have an office, so everybody was working remotely. As the number of views grew, they began spending more and more money with their own credit cards. They couldn't afford to keep it up the last month and desperately needed some funding. Chad and Steve still had a connection with Sequoia Capital, one of Silicon Valley's highly regarded venture capital firms from their PayPal days, and Sequoia Capital gave them $3.5 million for their first funding round.

YouTube's popularity was growing rapidly. Chad and Steve knew that they needed more cash for servers and hiring more people. While they were looking to raise more money, they were approached by Google and Yahoo; both of them were interested in buying YouTube. They met Google's team, including its co-founder Larry Page and CEO Eric Schmidt, at a Denny's because they didn't want anybody to know that they were talking to each other. It took about a week from the first conversation with Google to signing the actual contract. Google bought YouTube for $1.65 billion in October of 2006. YouTube was still less than two years old and had about 70 employees when the announcement came.

Since its purchase by Google, YouTube has expanded beyond the website into mobile apps, TV networks, and music. As of 2022, it is the second most visited website, with more than one billion monthly users. Steve and Chad left their roles at YouTube in 2010 but stayed as advisors for the company. After YouTube, Steve and Chad launched the startup AVOS Systems and another video-sharing application called MixBit. After 15 years of working together, Steve and Chad headed in different directions in 2014. While Chad kept working on MixBit, Steve went on to be an entrepreneur-in-residence at Google Ventures and moved back to Taiwan in 2019 with ambitions to help Taiwanese startups.

Chapter 40

Thanks to My Girlfriend

The Story of Zoom's Founder

"Your most unhappy customers are your greatest source of learning."
—*Bill Gates*

Z oom is a video conferencing platform used for virtual meetings, webinars, meeting recordings, and conducting live chats. The easy-to-use platform enabled people to virtually interact with co-workers and family members when in-person meetings weren't possible in 2020 after the coronavirus pandemic hit the world, earning Zoom global recognition. Now one of the leading video conferencing apps, Zoom was not considered an excellent idea when it was founded by Eric Yuan in 2011 in San Jose, California.

In 1987, Eric and his then-girlfriend attended different colleges in different cities in China. Back then, it was usually a nightmare to travel from one city to another. It was especially hard for Eric, who had to commute more than ten hours each trip. He had to take a crowded, foul-smelling overnight train to get to his girlfriend and take another train back home. During those trips, he wished he had a device to see his girlfriend and talk to her without having to travel all that way, which is when he started thinking about video calls.

After finishing his master's, Eric got his first job in 1991 as a software engineer. In 1994, he traveled from China to Japan for training for his work. Coincidently, Bill Gates was also there giving a speech on the internet. After hearing Bill Gates' speech, Eric realized that the internet would change everything. He saw a huge opportunity and decided to go to Silicon Valley in the United States to embrace the first wave of the internet revolution. Unfortunately, his application for a US visa was rejected.

Since he couldn't go to the US, Eric tried to start his small internet company in Beijing, China. However, almost nobody had heard about the internet in China back then, and he was convinced it would take another ten years for the internet to become well-known in his country. Eric didn't have the patience to wait for the internet to take off in China and wanted to move to the US as soon as possible. He applied for a US visa nine times until he finally got it in 1997. Erick gave up his own startup in China, hoping to establish one in the US, and directly moved to Silicon Valley.

Initially, Eric wanted to do sales or marketing jobs, but he did not know how to sell a product or even speak English properly. So, he had no choice but to become a programmer and write codes. After some time, he landed a job in Webex Communications and became their engineer number ten in 1997. Eric was a key player in developing Webex video conference software from the start and quickly rose in the ranks and became the VP of engineering. Webex became one of the first options for video calls in the market, and in 2007, it was acquired by Cisco for $3.2 billion. When Webex was sold to Cisco, it had 2800 employees and more than $800 million annual revenue.

Despite being very successful, Webex had several deficiencies, including unstable connectivity, lagging audio and video, and a frustrating installation process. At Cisco, Eric spent a lot of time talking with customers. He felt none of their customers were completely satisfied with Webex. So he was embarrassed that he had spent so much time building something that people did not like much. Eric then realized that Webex had been created to address old problems in video conferencing, while users' new demands in the smartphone era needed new solutions. But even as a corporate VP, he couldn't convince Cisco's upper management to make the next-generation solution. The company did not want to cannibalize its existing products and was focused more on enterprise software. Eric was determined to build something that both individual customers and enterprises would enjoy using. When he decided to start his own company to work on video calls, many of his friends told him that he had no chance in a super competitive space where Skype and other big companies were already present. But Eric knew that the customers were not satisfied with the existing solutions. He truly believed that he had a chance to make his customers happy with his new video conferencing tool because his goal was to create software that would solve all the new problems that didn't have a good solution.

When Eric left Cisco, 40 engineers on his team at Webex left with him too to join his new company, Zoom. In the beginning, Eric had trouble finding investors because many people thought the video tele-phony market was already saturated. So instead of venture capitalists, he raised money from his friends in 2011 and organized a team to start his idea. They worked very hard to build Zoom with a video-first mentality, while other companies like Skype had created audio first and then adjusted to video, a costly approach. In 2012, they launched a beta version of Zoom that could host video conferences with up to 15 participants. They started with a freemium business model, providing most of their service for free while other video conferencing providers charged their customers from the beginning. Zoom's customers could go to its website, set up a free account, and use it for free for 40 minutes, and if that 40-minutes was not enough for them, they could purchase a subscription.

For the first several months after releasing the beta version, they were excited every time they got a new paid subscriber. Some days they would get five new subscribers, which was considered huge. But if just one of those five people canceled their subscription, 20% of their sales would be gone. So, Eric would send out a personal email to every customer who canceled their service, and some of them replied. Eric would then schedule a call to understand why they canceled their service and promise to fix whatever problem they had experienced. After resolving some issues, beta testers were pleased with the product. After working for two years, the first version of Zoom was launched for the public in January 2013. From the start, it was massively successful, and just a few months later, Zoom had reached 1 million participants. By 2014, that number jumped to 10 million. Zoom was popular because it provided a lot for very little. The other secret to Zoom's popularity lay in the platform's ease of use, as users didn't need to have a Zoom account to attend a Zoom meeting.

In April 2019, Zoom became a public company. Typically, when tech companies hit the market, they're still burning significant amounts of cash, but Zoom was an exception: it was profitable. By the end of its first day of trading, Zoom's share price increased over 72%, giving the company a valuation of $16 billion. Since Eric owned a significant portion of Zoom, this made him a billionaire overnight.

When the COVID-19 global pandemic hit the world in 2020, it prompted an abrupt shift to remote work for many businesses worldwide. Suddenly there was a huge increase in Zoom usage for remote work, distance education, and online social relations. Many educational institutions switched to online classes using Zoom. Daily meeting participants rose from about 10 million in late 2019 to more than 300 million daily meeting participants in the spring of 2020. Despite facing increased competition by companies like Google, Facebook, Microsoft, and Cisco, Zoom has kept its momentum and is still one of the most popular video conferencing platforms worldwide.

About the Author

Sina Moeendarbari, PhD is a passionate tech entrepreneur and aspiring startup founder with a love of business and technology. Living in the heart of Silicon Valley, Sina has extensive experience as a Product and Technology Manager for Fortune 500 companies in the semiconductor world, and he has written numerous peer-reviewed papers in scientific journals. As the author of *Overnight or Over Time?* Sina has cultivated a deep understanding of the factors and talents behind the online world's biggest business tycoons, and he hopes to share these fascinating insights with a global audience to help like-minded tech enthusiasts.

Made in the USA
Middletown, DE
06 March 2022

62200315R00144